Stones of Evil

Also by Bryan Cooper:

The Ironclads of Cambrai
North Sea Oil – The Great Gamble
Battle of the Torpedo Boats
The Buccaneers
PT Boats
Alaska – The Last Frontier
Tank Battles of World War One
A History of Fighter Aircraft
A History of Bomber Aircraft
The E-Boat Threat
The Adventure of North Sea Oil
The War of the Gunboats
The Wildcatters

Stones of Evil

Bryan Cooper

.

Chapter One

Haril had been walking for more days than he could remember. Many times he had seen the moon grow big in the sky, then disappear like a woman when her hour has come and return as slender and fresh as a virgin to her marriage bed. He had trodden knee-high through snow and felt biting cold rain on his face and now the heat of summer sun was on his back. All the time he had kept to high ground, avoiding the forest that covered most of the low-lying land. The forest was dark and silent, often shrouded in the grey mist that rose from the dank undergrowth. It was the great unknown, into which his people rarely ventured, a place of danger and nameless fears that were spoken of in whispers around the village fires.

Only the hope that he might not be far from home gave Haril the strength to keep going. As if in a half-remembered dream there was a vague familiarity about the rolling chalky downs, the smell of gorse and heather and the springy turf beneath his feet. But he was weary to the point of exhaustion. His feet were blistered, his shoulders stooped under the weight of the leather pack. Most of all, he was hungry. For nearly a week now he had eaten nothing but wild berries; the few deer he had tried to stalk had always escaped into the forest before he was close enough to throw his spear.

All was quiet as he trudged on towards the ridge of the next hill. In the noon-day heat, every living being seemed to be at rest except himself. Even the birds had ceased their raucous aerial ballet. He was alone in the land.

And then he heard the scream.

It was thin and high-pitched, like an animal in pain. An animal being hunted perhaps. And hunting meant food. He stopped abruptly, straining his senses to locate the direction of the sound. It seemed to come from the other side of the hill. He eased the pack from his shoulders and holding it in one hand and his spear in the other, he ran at a crouching run up the slope, eager, but taking care to make no sound. When he neared the top he dropped to the ground and crawled the last few feet to peer cautiously over the crest of the hill.

He was looking across a broad, treeless plain. Far away on the other side there were more rolling hills that tugged at his memory as he realised that somewhere beyond them lay the sea. Then his attention was caught and held by a group of men standing some way down the slope below him. He was overjoyed to see they were his people. Most of them were young men like himself, sturdy and bearded, dressed in leather jerkins over knee-length woollen smocks and wearing thonged bear-hide sandals. They carried the same kind of flint spear and a lucky few had short bronze swords tucked into their belts. They stood sideways to him, grouped in a half-circle round a chalk pit. They were too far away for him to see what they were doing, but from their excited sounds he guessed they had trapped an animal.

Haril hesitated. For a man travelling alone, it was safer to avoid contact with people. He had discovered to his cost that not all communities lived in peace. And there were others, strange warriors who spoke a different tongue and roamed the land, fighting and pillaging. But Haril's hunger was sharper than ever, now that there seemed a chance of satisfying it. At least he had something to offer in return for their food.

Hoisting the pack over one shoulder he stood up, grasped his spear firmly, and strode down towards the men.

They were immediately aware of his appearance, silhouetted as he was against the sky. The shouting died away and they edged backwards in surprise. But when they saw he was alone a low growl arose and they angled their spears menacingly towards him.

'Peace to you and your people,' Haril called out hoarsely. It was strange to hear his voice again after so many days of silence and the sound startled him.

He was also uncomfortably aware of the pounding of his heart.

No one answered. He continued walking forward, smiling and trying to ignore their hostile stares. When he was about twenty lengths from the group, one of the men threw his spear. It thudded into the ground just ahead of Haril's feet. He stopped. What if he had made a mistake and they did not understand his words? He extended his right hand palm upwards in the traditional greeting.

An older man stepped towards him. He had grey hair and wore a cloak that was pinned below one shoulder with a large bronze buckle.

'If you speak our tongue, you know that we do not welcome strangers.' His voice grated harshly as he eyed Haril's travel-stained clothes and the dust and sweat that matted his beard.

Haril lifted the pack from his shoulder. 'I am a traveller and a worker of stone. See?'

He opened the pack and spilled its contents on to the ground. There were uncut flints, arrowheads, several small axes and the antler of a stag, shaped in the form of a hammer. These were the tools of his trade, a heavy burden to carry, but even in extreme exhaustion he had never considered casting them aside. His years of travelling, the very reason he left his village in the first place, would be meaningless without them. Better to die than face the contempt and laughter of those who had told him it was foolish to take up such a calling and to want to know what lay beyond the hills.

'I seek food and rest,' Haril said wearily. 'In return I will work the stone for you.'

The men pressed forward, murmuring among themselves and looking greedily at the implements. The older man smiled thinly. 'Our own people can do that.'

Haril guessed what was in his mind. It would be simple to kill him and take all the stones. 'Not this stone,' he said quickly. He bent down and picked up one of the uncut flints. Then he selected an ordinary arrowhead, placed it on one of the boulders that lay scattered over the ground, and struck it sharply with the flint. The arrowhead shattered but the flint was hardly scratched. Haril held it up for the men to see. They stared at it in amazement.

'It is stone from the mountains, far away from here. Only I can work it.'

The old man reached out and took the flint. He examined it carefully, rubbing his fingers over its smooth surface. 'I have heard of such stone.'

'It is the strongest stone there is,' Haril said. 'But it is difficult to shape.'

The old man weighed the flint thoughtfully in his hand.

'What are you called?'

'Haril.'

'And you have been to the mountains of the north?'

'Yes. And beyond them.'

There was a pause while the men whispered amongst themselves, darting furtive glances towards Haril. Then the old man spoke again. 'My name is Karn. I am the head of our village. Where are you from?'

Haril pointed to the distant hills. 'Where the white rocks stand against the sea, there is my village. And that is where I am going now.'

'Who is your head man?'

'I have been away for many times of the sun. But when I left, it was Thorin.'

One of the other men grunted. 'There was such a man. I have heard he is dead now.'

Haril felt a pang of sorrow as he remembered the kindly old man who had first taught him the skills of working stone and then encouraged him in his yearning to travel and see for himself the mysterious mountains of the north, against the opposition of his father and the others. So Thorin was in the long grave now, laid beside the other elders of the village.

Karn extended his arm towards Haril. 'You are welcome Haril. We accept your offer.'

With this greeting, the other men came crowding around Haril, fingering the flints. Their initial hostility had vanished. It was a rare enough event to see a stranger, let alone a worker of stone who had brought hard flint back from the mountains.

'There will be time at tonight's fire to hear the stranger's story,' Karn told them. He turned to Haril. 'Our village is not far. But first, we have a task to finish here.'

'I guessed you had been hunting,' Haril said, as casually as he could, picking up the flints and putting them into his pack.

Karn grinned. 'Hunting? Yes, we have been hunting.'

As he and the other men returned to where they had originally been standing, Haril had his first clear view of the chalk pit. The ground sloped downwards into a small quarry cut in the hillside. At the back was a chalk cliff which rose to a height of ten men. Generations of people had cut through the turf and taken away chunks of rock with which to build their huts. There was only one entrance to the quarry, since the cliff was too steep to climb, and this was now blocked by the men.

Halfway down the slope lay a tangled heap of dark skin and black hair. Haril could not recognise the animal. Behind it, vividly red against the powdery white chalk, was a trail of blood. Haril saw that while he and the men had been talking, the animal had crawled tortuously up the slope from the bottom of the quarry. It was not yet dead. Haril looked at it curiously. The figure moved slightly and with a sudden shock he saw that it was a man.

But no kind of man Haril had ever seen before. He was small in stature and had a low, protruding forehead. His head and much of his back and chest were covered in thick black hair. His naked skin was strangely pale except where blotched pink from a mixture of chalk dust and blood which oozed from many gaping wounds. As Haril watched, the man inched forward on his hands and elbows. His legs dangled broken and helpless behind him.

Meanwhile, Haril's new companions were picking up stones which lay scattered round the edge of the quarry. At a sign from Karn they began hurling them at the man in the pit. Some struck him on his head and body, making fresh wounds; others bounced along the ground and started a small landslide which took him slithering down to the bottom from where he had already crawled. The men laughed gleefully as he came to rest buried under a heap of stones. One of his arms clawed the air, grotesquely, as still he struggled to free himself. A cloud of chalk dust rose up from the quarry like smoke. All the time, Haril realised, the man had not made a sound.

But someone screamed. It was the same animal cry Haril had heard before. He turned and saw that two men in the group were clutching hold of a girl. She was yelling and struggling, desperate to free herself from their grasp. Her slight build and the long black hair which straggled wildly across her face showed her to be of the same race as the man in the quarry. But as Haril looked more closely he saw that her features were not greatly unlike those of the women of his own people. The eyes were set further apart perhaps, and the forehead was slightly lower. She wore an animal skin around her body, and as she fought the two men it was suddenly torn loose. Her naked body glistened with sweat and her skin was white. Although she stood no higher than Haril's chest, her firm rounded breasts revealed her to be fully grown. A roar of laughter went up from the men, which she answered with a shrill torrent of words in a tongue Haril had never heard before.

Karn was bending down and seemed to be searching the ground for something.

'Why?' Haril asked him. He had seen people stoned to death before. It was the penalty in some communities for a variety of offences – from lying with another man's wife to refusing an elder's command. But he could not imagine what these two strange beings had done.

Karn found what he wanted, a large rock that was the width of a man's body, and with a grunt picked it up in his powerful hands. 'They are from the forest,' he said.

A prickling sensation crawled over Haril's skin. He felt the same fear he had known as a child when he first heard whispers about the strange people who were said to haunt the forest. Later, with the arrogance of youth, he had dismissed such stories as old women's talk. It was obviously dangerous to go into the forest where animals could attack a man without warning. For that reason it seemed impossible that people could live there. And yet, as he stared at the girl, he knew that what Karn said must be true; it was only from the forest that such creatures could have come.

Holding the large rock, Karn walked slowly down the slope into the quarry. The others stopped shouting and watched him intently. By the time he reached the bottom, the forest-man had clawed a way for his head through the heap of stones, so he could breath. Karn lifted the rock high into the air, then looked round at his followers.

Quietly at first, in a whispered hiss, then gradually louder, they began to chant:

'Kill, kill, kill, kill...'

Over and over again until the rhythm of their voices shook the ground. Haril found himself shouting with them, hating these strange beings whom until now he did not believe existed. He wanted to be holding the rock himself. He wanted to crush that head with its black hair and low protruding forehead and staring eyes. And when, after standing motionless for several moments, Karn did bring the rock down with a sickening thud and the hairy skull cracked open and the arm no longer waved but dangled from the elbow like a broken stick, it was as if he himself had guided it to find its mark.

The girl had been screaming, but the sound was lost in the louder shouting of the men. Now, as silence fell with the final crushing blow of the rock, she gave a deep-throated groan and tore herself loose from her captors. With a swift, lithe movement she avoided their clutching hands and ran down the slope of the quarry, darting past Karn as he made his way out. She threw herself to her knees by the heap of stones and began to clear them away from the mangled body, all the time making strange moaning noises. Some of the men started to follow her, then changed their minds and picked up stones to throw at her. Blood flowed where they hit her body but she hardly seemed to be aware of it.

Karn lifted his arms and the stoning ceased.

'Tomorrow,' he called out. 'After we have shown her to our people.'

Two of the men went down to the girl. She spat and writhed as they tried to lift her away. One of them clenched his fist and clubbed her on the back of the neck. She fell to the ground, unconscious. Each taking an arm, they dragged her from the quarry. After a few steps, her heels left pink wet ruts in the chalk.

Led by Karn, the group turned away from the quarry and started off across the plain. High overhead, birds of prey were already beginning to gather, circling lower towards the promise of a fleshy feast. Rain clouds were building up over the distant hills. Haril fell into step beside the man who had known of Thorin. The blood-fever had left him now and he felt more exhausted than ever.

'Are they truly from the forest?' he asked.

The man glanced at him suspiciously. He had hawk-like features and a scar that ran all the way down one cheek.

'In all your travels, have you never seen them before?'

'No. I've heard stories. But – they spoke of devils.'

'They are devils.' The man lowered his voice and looked round nervously. 'When they come from the forest, our cattle give no milk, our crops wither and our children are born without life.'

Haril remembered times when such things had happened in his village and the women cried and beat their breasts, and the elders gave sacrifices to the spirits.

'None of our people ever saw them.'

'We have only seen them once before,' the man replied. 'And this is the first time we have captured any of them. That is why Karn is taking the girl to our village for the others to see.'

Haril glanced towards the girl who had partly recovered consciousness and, bound by leather thongs, was stumbling behind her captors. For a moment their eyes met and he was shocked to see that she was crying. He was reminded of his sister Sorin and the way she had looked when he went away from the village. She had been fourteen then, and that was four summers ago.

'Did you capture them in the forest?' he asked.

The man looked at him contemptuously. 'You take us for fools?'

'How then?'

'We were hunting bear. In the caves above the forest. That's where we found them.'

'Perhaps they were hunting too?'

'No.' Again the man lowered his voice. 'They were making devil-marks on the walls.'

'Devil marks? What are they?'

'It is better not to speak of such things.'

'But for that you put them to death by stoning?'

The man looked at him in amazement. 'What else would you do with them?'

Haril made no answer. His own community had always lived quietly and without violence, the men taking care of the cattle and sheep and sometimes hunting while the women tilled the fields. On the rare occasions when strangers came, a stone worker like himself perhaps or even, once, a worker of bronze, they were immediately made welcome. The stories they told would be repeated round the fire long after they had left. But little else ever happened to disturb the routine pattern of living as season followed season and children were born and old people died. It was in fact the monotony of this unchanging way of life that had made Haril restless to see other places and become a traveller himself, the first to leave his village for as long as anyone could remember. It was then he found that the ways of others were not always so peaceful and he realised how much his people owed to the wise and gentle guidance of Thorin. The time had come when he longed for the peaceful security of his own village and he felt the need to see his family again, his father and mother, his brother Torm and little Sorin. He would bring them the new skills he had learned and they would be proud of him, especially his father who had been so against him leaving in the first place.

It was on such thoughts and memories that he mused as the group made its way silently across the plain, and it came as a sudden surprise when they reached the village and he found it was already late afternoon. The village, unlike his own, was surrounded by a wooden stockade built on top of an earth embankment. In the fields outside, women were tilling crops of wheat and barley; they stood up and stared as the group approached, but made no rush to welcome the men as might have been expected. Their expressions were surly and withdrawn. As the group came nearer, they left their work and drifted silently in its wake. Haril saw it was not a happy village.

A section of the stockade was lowered and the men climbed the path over the embankment and entered the village. Haril saw it was like many others he had visited. The huts were built of mud and stone with peat roofs; old women squatted outside some of them, pounding grain in large earthen bowls or rubbing and twisting tufts of grey wool in their hands to make a continuous thread. Naked children ran about the open compound, darting amongst the pigs and chickens which roamed everywhere. As a stranger, Haril expected to be the usual object of curiosity and he was prepared for the usual questions, even though all he wanted now was food and rest. But as the women and the other men who had not been on the hunting party gathered round them, it was the girl who attracted most of their attention. A very old woman, her face weathered and wrinkled like the bark of a tree, hobbled forward and pointed a bony finger.

'Who is she?'

Karn, proud and arrogant, looked round at the assembled people. 'She is from the forest,' he announced loudly.

There was a moment of utter silence, then a long drawn-out hiss. The women began to edge away from the girl and Haril was surprised at the hatred that came to their eyes until he remembered his own feeling at the chalk pit. Seeing it in others made him wish that he had not been there. Karn explained what had happened, then gave an order for the girl to be taken to one of the huts. The women followed, spitting and hissing but keeping well away from her. The children, pleased at the unexpected excitement, danced among them, jeering and throwing handfuls of dirt at her.

The old woman grumbled: 'They go after bear-meat which we need for the winter. And all they bring back is this wretched girl. What brave hunters.'

But no one took any notice of her.

When the girl had been locked in the hut, Karn came over to Haril. People were now beginning to take notice of this other stranger who had come into their midst, but Haril saw that it was mostly suspicion in their eyes and not curiosity. The hunters were whispering amongst themselves and glancing at him.

'Now you will show us the hard stone and how it is cut,' Karn said.

'I need food and rest first.'

Karn frowned. 'Very well. Tonight you will sit with us round the fire. And tomorrow you will work the stone.'

Haril followed him across the compound to one of the larger huts. It was dark inside and smelled of animals and earth. As soon as Karn had left, Haril threw himself down on the furs that were scattered over the earthen floor. He felt numb from tiredness. When Karn returned with a woman carrying a bowl of stewed meat, he was asleep.

'Shall I wake him?' the woman asked.

Karn stood for a moment looking down at him, then shook his head. 'Leave the food there.'

The woman placed the bowl beside Haril. 'How long will he be with us?'

Karn laughed softly. 'For as long as he has skills to teach us.'

'And then?'

'Perhaps we shall let the women decide.'

The woman grinned and followed Karn out of the hut. Haril groaned in his sleep and turned over, his face burrowing into the warm fur.

Chapter Two

Haril woke with an aching body and no clear memory of where he was. He lay without moving, his senses instinctively alert. The smells that came to him were not familiar, neither was the darkness after sleeping for so many nights in the open and waking to the chill morning light and the sound of birds. Gradually, he remembered. He blinked his eyes and the darkness became shadows which flickered strangely on the walls. He looked towards the narrow entrance of the hut and saw an orange glow framed by the doorway. It was still night and there was fire outside.

Hunger gnawed at him like a pain. He sat up and traced the smell of meat to the bowl that lay beside him. The meat was cold now, congealed in its own fat, but he ate ravenously, scooping out every last morsel with his fingers. The he lay back on the fur and would have slept again. But the glow from outside was suddenly blocked off as a figure stood in the entrance and there was a new light as Karn entered with a guttering torch held above his head.

'We wish to talk with you,' he commanded gruffly.

Haril struggled to his feet and almost fell down again as his knees sagged weakly. It was against all the laws of hospitality not to allow a traveller full rest before making his appearance at the fire.

'You are indeed eager to hear my words,' he said contemptuously.

Karn's jaw tightened, but when he spoke, his voice was even and controlled. 'It is a long time since a stranger was here. We would know of other people and other places.'

He turned and stooped to make his way through the narrow entrance. Haril followed him.

A large fire was burning in the middle of the compound. The flames had died down to a red glow and Haril could see it had been alight for some time. The men squatted round it in a circle, their arms resting on their knees. Behind them sat the women, some of them holding children to their breasts. Away from the fire, the sod huts were bathed in pale moonlight. There were many stars in the dark roof of the sky, pin-points of silver light where it was said the giant Raven had thrust his beak in trying to escape when the god of night netted him with his cloak. Haril remembered nights like this among his own people, those special times before everyone lay down to sleep, when the old stories were retold and men spoke freely of the things they had seen and of other stranger things that had come into their minds.

Then Haril saw something that was not like his own village and which immediately drove away all memory of it. To one side of the fire was a large post, embedded firmly into the ground. Tied to it and sagging against the thongs that bound her was the dark girl from the forest. She was still naked and as Haril passed by, he smelt the acrid odour of burnt flesh. Her eyes were closed and she was motionless, as if in sleep. He saw savage burn marks on her arms and breasts. He wondered if she had screamed and he had been too tired to wake, or whether she had made no sound like her companion.

The men moved round the fire to make room for him. He sat between Karn and a very old man with wizened grey skin and white hair.

'The traveller who comes in peace is welcome,' the old man muttered, not looking at Haril but gazing into the fire where he seemed to see things that others could not. Perhaps he did, for he was blind. His thin voice was like the rustle of dry leaves in the breeze.

Karn looked round at the circle of faces. 'This is Haril. He is a worker of stone and he has been to the mountains of the north.'

There was a low murmur from the assembly. A young man of about Haril's age stared at him across the fire. 'How many travelled with you?'

'I went alone,' Haril replied.

'But you are no warrior. You do old man's work with your making of stone.'

'If I am an old man, then you are a child who still suckles at his mother's breast.'

The young man sprang angrily to his feet, but Karn waved him down. 'Be still.' He turned to Haril. 'Tell us about the mountains.'

Haril looked contemptuously at the men as they waited for his words. They were like others in the few isolated villages he had come across in his travels. Never had they been further from their homes than the distance a hunter could carry a deer he had killed; they feared anything they could not see or which lay beyond their own hills. Many were not even hunters any longer, now they had learned to breed cattle and sheep that would not stray and had found ways of growing food in the fields. It would be a great event for any of them to visit one of the neighbouring villages and few would have done even that.

'The mountains are many days from here,' he began slowly. 'It was a long and perilous journey to avoid the great forest, which is everywhere. At night, the wolves and bears would come and only my fire kept them from attacking me. Once, I came upon a she-bear with her cubs. It was a long fight. I wounded her with my arrows but still she came at me. I have the marks of her claws on my body. But at last I got my spear into her neck and killed her.'

He had their attention now. They were leaning forward, staring at him. Several muttered wonderingly, but he saw there was disbelief on the faces of some of the others.

'The skin is in my pack,' he added.

'It was a brave fight,' one of them said. Haril recognised him as the scarred hunter he had spoken with before. The others nodded and Haril felt warmed by their admiration.

'There were great rivers which I had to cross on the logs of fallen trees. And I saw a bird that was big enough to carry a sheep. And strange animals with hair on their necks and long tails, eating grass like your cattle.'

Scarface nodded. 'I too have seen such animals. But never birds like that. Perhaps it was the Raven who fights the cloak of night.'

The others looked at one another uneasily.

'I don't think so,' Haril said. 'It wasn't black but brown and gold, like the sun shining on the trees when the leaves change their colour.'

There was a long silence. One of the women came forward and threw wood on the fire. Flames licked the chill night air. A child mewed softly, then went to sleep again under the caress of his mother.

'Did you see people?' Karn asked.

'Yes. At first, on the high ground, a few villages such as this. I lived in one when the time of the cold came and snow covered the land. And then, until I reached the mountains, there was nothing but the great forest. But on my way back from the mountains – there were others.'

'What others?'

Haril hesitated. He did not yet understand what he had seen. And if he did not, then how would these ignorant farmers, who had been nowhere and seen nothing? He regretted his words but it was too late to go back on them now.

'Once, I slept in a tree because it was raining and I couldn't make a fire. I woke to see them passing below me. They were big men. Giants. Every one carried a bronze sword and a shield. They spoke words that I had never heard before.'

He did not add that he had been more frightened than at any time in his life. He looked round the circle to see what effect his words might have had. But no one moved, no one spoke.

'One other time I saw them, from a long way off. They came from a village like this, which was burning. Their swords flashed brightly, like the flames. I didn't stay to see more.'

Karn nodded gravely. 'We have heard of such people.'

'Who are they?'

'Where they come from, we do not know. But they have no friendship for our people. They kill. But enough of that. Tell us more of the mountains.'

Haril wanted to talk more of the strange invaders, but he saw he would get nothing from Karn. He closed his eyes and brought into his mind a picture of the mountains as they were when he first saw them.

'From a long way off, they are like clouds at the edge of the sky,' he murmured, still keeping his eyes closed. 'As I came near they rose higher and higher until I had to lean my head back to see the top of them. And when I began to climb, there were even higher mountains beyond. There were some so high that they pierce the roof of the sky and you cannot see the top of them. And even in the sun it is cold and there is snow in the high places and to drink the water in the streams is like a knife thrust into your chest.'

He opened his eyes. The men were staring at him in wonderment.

'And that is where the hard flint comes from?' Karn said.

Haril nodded. He remembered the first time he had held the hard stone in his hands. It was cold and unyielding, heavy with strength. He loved all kinds of stone, the soft, gritty sandstone that required gentle fingers to shape, the granite boulders that had to be struck in just the right place or they would shatter into useless fragments. But the hard flint from the mountains that gave so reluctantly to the chipping of his axe was the most exciting of all.

'Do you find it in the fields as we do when we dig the earth?' one of the men asked.

Haril laughed. 'There are no fields. The mountains are all rock. The flint comes from mines.'

Karn looked puzzled. 'Mines?'

'Holes made in the ground.' Haril felt impatient. He was tired again, and bored at the ignorance of his listeners. 'They go down to the height of many men.'

'It must take a long time to make such a hole,' Karn said.

'Too long for the lifetime of any one man.'

'I don't understand.'

'You don't imagine I could do such work alone, do you?'

The young hunter who had spoken earlier glared at Haril and spat angrily into the fire. 'So you did have followers with you.'

'No. The people who mine the flint showed me where to find it and how to shape it into axes and arrows.'

The men frowned, only slowly understanding what the words meant. Karn turned to Haril. 'You mean, people live in the mountains?'

'Of course. Just as you farm the land, they take stone from the mountains. They have done so for longer than any of them can remember.'

As he spoke, Haril looked round at the circle of men facing him and saw the shock that his words had caused. Their eyes opened wide in amazement.

And there was also a sense of fear that Haril could feel as an almost tangible presence. It was fear of the unknown, of something outside their comprehension. They muttered uneasily amongst themselves. Only the very old man remained unmoved. He continued to stare into the fire with his blind eyes.

Haril smiled to himself, both amused and contemptuous, forgetting his own astonishment when he had first discovered the miners' settlements. It was only later after he had been welcomed by them as a brother stone worker, that he had come to know them as friends. They knew more about stone than he had ever dreamed possible and had shown him their secrets. They were proud of their knowledge and were happy to share it with any who came in peace. They also had an inner wisdom of the ways of man that had made Haril feel as ignorant as the peasants who were now before him. He wished he could have asked the mining people about the strange invaders, but he had not seen them until after he had left the mountains and by that time he was on his way home.

'It's hard to believe that people live at the very edge of the world,' Karn murmured.

There was a note of doubt in his voice that angered Haril. He spoke harshly, forgetting his caution. 'The edge of the world? That is a foolish thought.'

'It's known that the world is bounded on one side by the sea and on the other side by the mountains.' Karn's voice hardened. At any other time Haril would have been warned by it and held his peace. But now he was determined to show these simple people how little they knew.

'I don't know where the world ends,' he said. 'But it is not at the mountains. Beyond them there is more land. And then the sea. And beyond the sea there are other lands.'

'Other lands?' Karn whispered as if afraid to say the words out loud.

'Yes. Men come to trade with the miners for flint. They bring copper and tin and strange fruits to eat. I have seen them, and the round logs they use to carry them over the water. And I have heard...'

'You lie.' One of the men jumped to his feet and pointed his finger at Haril.

Others stood up, shouting and shaking their fists at Haril. He regretted now the impulse to boast, but it was too late.

'Listen to me,' he shouted. 'What I have said is true.' He started to get up but the men were now gathered round him and hands reached out and roughly pushed him down again. Only Haril and Karn and the old man were still seated on the ground. The shouting became louder.

'We know from the priests there is nothing beyond the mountains,' cried one.

'The stranger mocks us,' shouted another.

'He is not of our people.'

'Our enemies sent him.'

'Death to the stranger.'

At this last cry, the old man turned to face the crowd. It might have been the firelight glinting in his sightless eyes, the pupils pointing upwards and almost hidden under his eyelids so that only white showed in the sockets, but there was something about him that compelled attention. His voice was scarcely louder than a whisper, yet all heard him.

'Listen to the stranger,' he said. 'There are many things we do not know. None of us have seen beyond the mountains. How do we know what he says is untrue?'

There was a moment's silence. Then the young hunter pushed his way forward.

'The only one who believes the stranger is the blind man,' he shouted with a harsh laugh. 'He cannot see anything, yet he will tell you what is true or false.' He thrust his hand out and held up three fingers in front of the old man's face. 'What do you see, old man?'

'I see the jealousy in your heart,' the old man replied quietly.

The hunter laughed again. 'No one can see a man's heart until it is cut from him. The years have made you foolish, old man.' He turned to the others.

'This stranger seeks power over us by making us afraid. But it is he who must fear. He must die.'

A great roar of assent greeted these words. Haril felt himself grabbed and hauled to his feet by a dozen eager hands. Just as he was being dragged away from the fire, Karn held up both arms. 'You may kill the stranger,' he shouted.

'Yes, yes,' chorused the voices.

'But if you do, you will go hungry this winter,' Karn's deep voice echoed loudly round the walls of the settlement. 'If that is what you wish, do your will.'

There was a murmur of puzzlement from the men. 'We don't understand,' said one.

'Have you forgotten? The stranger is to teach us how to work the hard stone.'

'He has lied and blasphemed,' shouted another.

'Words, words,' Karn growled contemptuously. 'Are they more important than stronger arrows and spears? Better hunting and death to our enemies? We shall have these things with the stranger's help. But not if you kill him.'

The men looked doubtfully at one another.

'Karn is right,' one of them called out, and Haril saw it was Scarface. 'It is better to have these weapons.'

'Let the stranger go,' Karn ordered.

Reluctantly, the men released their hold on Haril.

'Now go to your homes and let us have no more talk of death.'

Slowly, glancing suspiciously at Haril but with their anger dissipated, they began to drift away. Only the young hunter remained where he stood, glaring at Haril with hatred in his eyes. Karn moved towards him, reaching for the sword by his side.

'Do you refuse to obey me?'

The young man hesitated, then he too turned abruptly and disappeared into the darkness.

'I apologise for my son,' Karn said, coming over to Haril and standing beside him. 'And the others. They are like children who fear anything they do not know.'

'You saved my life,' said Haril shakily.

Karn smiled and put his hand on Haril's shoulder. 'Then you will forgive us?'

'It was foolish of me to talk as I did.'

'And you will stay as our guest until you are strong enough to travel again? There'll be no more trouble, I promise you.'

Haril glanced round the compound. All was quiet now. Only the old man still sat by the dying embers of the fire. Haril believed what Karn said. He also knew that what had happened was largely his fault, and yet this village made him uneasy.

'Perhaps we may speak of it tomorrow,' he said hesitantly.

'Certainly. And now – come. I'll take you back to your hut.'

Karn moved away. Haril was about to follow when he found that one of his sandals was missing, apparently pulled off in the struggle. So much had happened that he had not noticed it before. He looked around and saw it lying on the ground beside the fire, close to the old man. Calling out to Karn to wait for him, he went over to pick it up. As he bent down, the old man spoke. His voice was so quiet that Haril could barely hear the words.

'Do not trust Karn,' the old man whispered. He remained absolutely motionless, staring into the fire. 'Leave this place.'

Haril froze in the act of tying the sandal to his foot. He slowly turned but already the old man had risen to his feet.

'It is time you went to your rest, old man,' Karn called out impatiently.

The old man nodded and shuffled away without another word. His legs were bowed where the bones had softened. Haril stood watching him, wondering at the words he had spoken. And he also wondered at the coincidence of the missing sandal. Had the old man taken it on purpose?

Haril was suddenly aware that Karn was standing next to him.

'Are you interested in the old man?' Karn asked, and Haril sensed a note of suspicion in his voice.

'I was thinking he must be very old,' he replied carefully.

'Older than even he can remember,' Karn said. 'He was our headman once. Now his time has almost come. His grandson has a place waiting for him.'

Haril understood. It was the custom for a young couple to bury the body of a respected member of the family in a crouching position under the wall of their marriage home, so that his spirit would hold up the stones and protect them from harm. Haril remembered when his own grandfather had died and was buried in a corner of the room near the hearth. As a child it was always to that place he ran when he was in any kind of trouble. It had given him a warm feeling of comfort. What Karn said sounded so natural and he was so friendly when he saw Haril back to the hut and wished him a peaceful night that later, lying on the floor in a vain attempt to sleep, Haril wondered if his suspicions were wrong. He could have been mistaken about what the old man said. Or maybe the old man was strange in the head and did not know what he was saying. It happened with old people sometimes. But still he could not get the words out of his mind.

After moving restlessly from one side to another, the time came when Haril knew he would get no more sleep that night. He sat up. The large circular hut was in complete darkness. Only a few streaks of moonlight showed through cracks in the wooden door. He crawled over and put his eye to the largest gap. Outside, the moon was still casting a pale light over the compound. A few lengths from the hut, seated on the ground and looking as if he might be nodding off to sleep, was one of the hunters, armed with spear and sword. A guard to protect Haril just in case anyone tried to attack him, Karn had said. It sounded reasonable. But it also occurred to Haril that the man might be on watch to prevent him leaving.

There was only one way to find out. There was no reason why he should not leave the hut for a few moments to get fresh water. He would test the guard's reaction. He pushed the door to open it. And it was then that he discovered it would not move. It was locked from the outside. He was no longer a guest, but a prisoner.

The realisation of his danger and of the urgent need to do something about it brought all Haril's senses to a fine pitch of alertness. The last vestiges of tiredness left him and he felt almost exhilarated at the thought of action ahead, however it might end. From what he had already seen of this village, he knew he could expect little mercy if he tried to escape and was caught. But if he did stay, he could also guess what his fate would be once he had shown them how to work the hard stone. Haril decided to take his chances now, when, hopefully, they would think he was off his guard.

He crawled back across the floor to where his pack lay and quietly emptied it on to the floor. Carefully feeling the flints, one by one, he selected a few of the hardest and sharpest. The others, together with his tools and the pack itself, he would have to leave behind.

One of the flints he had chosen was already shaped into a spearhead. Taking hold of this he stood up and made his way to that part of the wall furthest away from the door. The roof sloped down to join the top of the wall at shoulder level. By reaching between the wooden beams that supported the roof, Haril could dig under the peat covering. It had been baked hard by the sun, but gradually began to crumble with the pounding of the flint. Earth and peat trickled down to make a steadily increasing mound at his feet until at last one of his thrusts broke through and there was a small hole in the roof through which he could see the night sky. It did not take long to widen this until it was big enough for him to crawl through. But he still had the problem of the wooden beams underneath, which were spaced at intervals the width of an outstretched hand. He tried pulling them apart, but they were too firmly held in place by the weight of the roof. He was sweating and panting from his exertions by now, and frustrated at seeing the means of escape barred like a cage.

He sat down to think. If he cut through one of the beams there was a danger that part of the roof might collapse. But there seemed no other way. Reaching back to select the sharpest of the flints, he began sawing at the wood. It was slow, laborious work, for he could not chop at it like an axe because of the noise he would make. But at last the wood began to creak and split open. Standing so that the upper length would rest on his shoulder when it broke, he continued to saw carefully. Suddenly the beam gave way, and its weight on Haril's shoulder bent him almost double.

He knelt down, took old of the beam and eased it to the ground. Chunks of peat thudded down onto the floor, but most of it stayed in place, sagging between the gap. Haril quickly picked up the flints he had selected and put them into the pouch of his jerkin, then grasped the beams on either side of the hole he had made and pulled himself up on to the roof. Swinging his legs out and over the side of the hut, he dropped soundlessly to the ground.

All was quiet in the village. He crept round the hut until he could see across the compound. The guard still sat there, motionless. Haril had calculated that the gate in the stockade lay to the right. He could reach it by circling round, mostly keeping behind the other huts. Taking a deep breath, he stepped away from the protective shelter of his own hut.

Suddenly there was a loud thud from inside. More of the sagging roof had fallen down. Haril froze, for a second undecided whether to go back or carry on. But it was too late either way. The guard could not have been completely asleep for he was on his feet and turning round almost at once. Haril stood before him in the full light of the moon.

For the time of several heartbeats, the two men faced each other. Then, with a growl, the guard took a step forward and hurled his spear at Haril.

Haril did the only thing possible, which was to drop flat to the ground. He felt the shoulder of the spearhead graze past his ear as he fell. Then the guard was coming at him with his sword raised. Desperately rolling on to his side Haril reached for one of the flints. Just as the guard was about to strike, Haril threw the flint with all the strength he could muster. It caught him in the throat and it must have been the sharp side for blood suddenly spurted out and he fell to the ground without making any sound through his sliced windpipe.

Haril jumped to his feet, his heart pounding against his ribs, and ran back to the side of the hut. He pressed himself against the wall, listening tensely to see if the disturbance had woken anyone. Somewhere at the other side of the village a dog barked. But that was the only sound. Even the barking stopped after a while and all was silent once more. Stealthily, Haril crept over to retrieve the piece of flint from where it lay near the body of the guard, and moved on to cross the now deserted compound.

Or was it deserted? At the very moment when he was congratulating himself that he had a good chance of escaping, he suddenly felt he was being watched.

He turned slowly, holding the flint tightly in his hand, afraid of what he might see. Karn perhaps, with a mocking smile on his lips, or the young hunter who was his son, about to rend Haril with his spear.

But it was the dark-haired girl. Still tied to the post, she was staring at Haril with wide open eyes. He sighed with relief, and was about to continue on across the compound when the thought came to him that she had only to cry out to give him away. That is, if they had not cut out her tongue already. He stepped towards her, his arm drawn back and ready to throw the flint if she opened her mouth to shout. But she just looked at him without expression. It would be a quicker death this way than at the hands of Karn and his men. Haril felt no hatred for her, only the sympathy he would have for any ill-treated animal. Having now seen the forest people at close quarters he wondered why his people had always been so afraid of them. But he could not take the

risk that she might give him away. After all, he was
of the same race as those who persecuted her, even
though he was now their enemy as well. He stood in
front of her, gripped the flint like a knife and raised
it toward her throat. And all the time her eyes never
left his and it was as if she knew what he was about
to do and accepted it.

Or was there something else in those dark,
fathomless eyes? Afterwards, he was never quite
sure. There was pain, certainly, although never once
did the slightest sound escape her compressed lips.
But there was also a sense of power and a strange
compulsion that seemed to burn into his mind and
awaken memories of ancient ways long forgotten.
Whatever it was, something made him change his
mind at the last moment. With the flint poised in
mid-air about to strike, he suddenly brought it down
and cut the thongs that bound her to the post. She
fell forward and would have collapsed to the ground
had he not caught her in his arms.

He held her upright while the strength slowly
returned to her body and as he waited he silently
cursed himself for having acted like a fool. He was
wasting precious time. It was already beginning to
get light and at any moment someone might see
them. And the girl, wounded and weakened as she
was, could only make his escape more difficult. But
he was also aware of a quickened heart-beat and a
stirring in his blood as he felt the touch of her naked

body against his and the softness of her hair as she clung to him for support.

After a while she pulled away from him, staggered a few steps, then stood upright and signalled to him by a nod that she was ready to leave. He pointed across the compound and together, glancing cautiously from side to side, they crept forward.

As Haril expected, the gate in the stockade was closed. It had been pulled up and was now held in place by two ropes which went over the top of the stockade and down to where the ends were looped round pegs in the ground. It could be lowered from the inside by unhitching the ropes and walking forward until the gate was lying flat. Haril had intended to climb over the top of it, but he could see from the girl's painful movements that she would not have the strength for such an effort. They would have to lower the gate. He indicated his intention to the girl. Each of them took hold of a rope, then at his signal they pulled them off the pegs. At first the weight on the ropes was not unduly heavy. But as they edged slowly forwards and the gate hinged down from a vertical to a horizontal position, its weight gradually increased until they were both straining back to prevent it falling. Then their feet began slipping on the smooth, dusty ground. Haril looked desperately around for something to hold on to, but there was nothing. The girl panted desperately as she strove to take her share of the weight. Suddenly, with a small cry, her feet slithered forwards and she fell on to her back. The extra weight that was transferred to Haril snatched the rope from his hands. The gate fell down with a loud clatter.

There was no time to think. Again, in the village, dogs had started to bark. A man's voice called out sleepily. Haril turned to help the girl but already she had picked herself up from the ground. He grabbed her arm and together they ran through the opening in the stockade, down the earth embankment, and away from the village across the dew-wet grass of the plain. Haril had no idea where to head for. Individual features in the misty landscape were beginning to take shape in the grey light of dawn, but this was unknown country to Haril. He was vaguely aware that the girl appeared to be guiding them in a particular direction and he obeyed without protest. They had not covered a distance greater than the flight of an arrow before a loud clamour arose from the village. Their escape had already been discovered. Even as Haril glanced desperately back over his shoulder, the first men appeared in the gateway. Shouting and brandishing spears they streamed out of the village and across the plain in pursuit, running with the loping gait of practised hunters.

Had Haril been alone, he might have been able to out-run them. Had the girl been fit even, they might have stood a chance. But certainly not in her present condition, tired and obviously in considerable pain. She struggled bravely but gradually her strides became shorter and slower and Haril found himself having to fall back so that she could keep up with him. Once having made the decision to help her, it did not occur to him to abandon her and take his chances alone.

The noise of their pursuers grew louder and Haril knew it could only be a short time before they were caught. He hoped that, in the excitement and triumph of the chase, they would make their kill quickly. Already he could hear arrows whispering through the air and the dull thud of spears falling to the ground behind them. It was not long before the first one, then another arrow flew past them as they came within bowshot. Suddenly, Haril felt a searing pain as one embedded itself in his shoulder, thrusting him forward so that he staggered to his knees and nearly fell. As he forced himself to his feet, aware of the blood streaming warmly down his back, he glanced behind him and had a fleeting impression of triumphant faces and shouts coming from mouths strained wide open, and an expression of hatred and anticipation on one face in particular, that of the young hunter who was Karn's son.

Haril turned to make one last, hopeless effort, his head swimming from exhaustion and loss of blood. It was then that he became dimly aware that the girl was leading him towards the edge of the dark forest. He instinctively began to veer away in another direction but she tugged urgently at his arm and shouted strange words. A black cloud was settling over him so that he could hardly see and the waves of pain were so intense that nothing seemed to matter much anyway. He stumbled along, half-dragged by the girl, and vague images came to him as if from a great distance. Shadows emerged from the trees, the ground trembled with the tread of running feet, there were loud shouts and blurred movements. The last thing Haril knew as the blackness finally overcame him and he sank unconscious to the ground was the feeling of many hands grasping eagerly for his body and savage faces pressed close to his.

Chapter Three

A priest had once told Haril of an ancient belief that the spirit could leave the body when it was asleep. Dreams were merely vague memories of what had taken place in another existence. And that was how Haril remembered the forest people and the days he spent with them when the fever was upon him. His mind drifted continually in and out of consciousness so that, afterwards, he was never quite certain what had been real and what was only imagined.

Some recollections stood out clearly. There was a long journey through the forest, being carried on the shoulders of swarthy little men with long dark hair and fierce eyes. Leaves that were cool and heavy with summer brushed against his face and body. Then there was pain and more darkness. And every so often there was a soft couch of sweet-smelling herbs and gentle hands touching the wound on his shoulder. A bitter liquid was poured into his mouth and he fell back asleep where there was no more pain. It seemed that he woke sometimes and there was a blurred impression of strange shapes and colours and flickering firelight and many faces peering at him. The one who gave him the liquid that brought such peace and tranquillity was the girl he had rescued. He thought he glimpsed the face of one of his own people but he could not be sure that it was not part of his dream. He was certain of one thing, however. He knew they were trying to help him. As the fever gradually left him and the strength flowed back into his limbs, the shapes around him became more substantial and questions formed in his mind. But always, the liquid eased him back into sleep and forgetfulness.

Except once. He woke as usual, drowsy and sluggish, but suddenly his mind cleared and he remembered all that had happened up to the time he was wounded. He struggled to sit up and was shocked to find how weak his body had become. Slowly, experimentally, he stretched his arms and legs. They were stiff but he was thankful that the wound in his shoulder had healed. He lay back, exhausted. As his eyes became accustomed to the semi-darkness, he saw that he was in a large cave. From the damp, musty smell he knew it must be some way underground. A fire glowed to one side of him, its smoke escaping through a crack in the rock. As he stared up at the roof of the cave which was not far above him, the flames spluttered and flared for a moment as they caught a piece of dry wood, and in the brighter light he saw something that made him tense every muscle of his body.

The ceiling was covered with richly coloured paintings of animals, roughly shaped to the undulations of the rock. Some were standing still with heads bowed and arrows sticking in their flanks, others were running in flight with naked men chasing them. The colours were so vivid and the simple outlines so lifelike that the whole ceiling seemed to be alive with movement. Some of the animals Haril could recognise, like the deer and bison and goats with curved horns. But there were other strange shapes that he had never seen before. Huge creatures with long tusks and hairy bodies and even weirder two-legged beings with large round heads that seemed to be floating rather than standing on the ground like the others.

For a long time Haril stared at the pictures, stirred by their beauty. If he half closed his eyes it was not difficult to imagine that he, too, was out on the plains, hunting with the other men. Then the fire died down and the pictures faded and there were just grey shadows on the rock so that it might have been no more than one of his dreams. There was a movement by his side. He turned and saw the dark-haired girl approaching with a small cup in her hand, filled with the bitter liquid he had come to know so well. She bent over him and lifted it towards his lips. He shook his head.

'No – no more,' he whispered.

The girl glanced over her shoulder. A vague shape was huddled by the fire: an old woman so thin and fragile, her wrinkled skin so white, that she seemed to be more shadow than substance. The girl spoke to her in strange tongue. She remained motionless for a moment, then rose to her feet and came slowly towards them. She was wearing a long garment of some silken material that was unlike anything Haril had ever seen before; it was much finer and softer than the rough woollen clothes of his own people. The girl wore the same kind of garment except that it was cut short just below her knees.

'The liquid will bring the strength back to your body,' the old woman said in a thin, high-pitched voice. She spoke in Haril's own language.

'And make me sleep,' Haril replied tersely.

'Yes, that too.'

'How long have I lain here?'

'For nearly one time of the moon, as you would call it.'

Haril lay back on the couch, his mind a jumble of confused thoughts.

'You speak our tongue,' he murmured wonderingly.

'Some of us do. It is well sometimes to be able to understand the words of your enemy.'

'We are not your enemies,' Haril protested, but even as he spoke he remembered the way Karn and his men had treated the girl and he felt a pang of apprehension at what her revenge might be.

'Not you, perhaps. You saved Zia, and for that, I thank you. Zia is the daughter of my daughter and

50

very precious to me.' The old woman smiled fondly at the girl.

'Mogan is very kind.' The girl spoke slowly and hesitantly in Haril's language. He stared at her in surprise.

'You too? Why didn't you speak so in the village?'

The girl gave him a long, hard look. 'Would that have helped? Or would Karn have hated me even more and made my death even slower.'

Haril remembered the pit and shuddered. He hoped the girl had not seen his own reactions to the stoning. 'Who was the man they ... killed?' he asked.

'My brother.'

'I am sorry. Truly.'

The girl's eyes flashed angrily. 'Your people are evil.'

'Karn has poisoned the minds of his people. But not all villages are like that.'

'They are devils,' the girl continued, as if he had not spoken.

'They say the same about you.'

'Do we torture and kill your kind?'

Haril felt the anger rising within him. 'It is said you cast spells on our women when they are in childbirth,' he retorted.

The girl laughed harshly. 'Are your people so foolish they believe in such things?'

Haril frowned, hardly knowing how to answer. He himself had always doubted some of the stories whispered round the fire. But he was relieved of the necessity to speak by the old woman who stepped between them, her hand raised. 'Be quiet,' she commanded. 'There is not much time before our guest must leave.'

Haril looked up at her. 'You would let me go, then?'

'Zia speaks angry words. But she knows it is not our custom to harm a guest. Is that not so?' She turned to the girl who had withdrawn into the shadows where Haril could not see her. For one moment he wondered if even now she was taking out a knife to strike him. A cold sweat broke out on his forehead. But when she reappeared he saw that she had only picked up the cup of liquid.

'Morgan is right,' she said softly. 'You were kind to me and for that I thank you. And now, you must drink.'

'I do not wish to sleep,' Haril protested.

'It is necessary.'

The old woman nodded. 'We do not wish even you to see where we live. While you sleep, our men will take you to the edge of the forest. You will not know how to find your way back.'

'Why should I want to?'

'To bring Karn and his hunters.'

Haril flushed indignantly. 'I would not do such a thing. They are my enemies too.'

'But if they caught you and put fire to your body,' Zia said quietly, 'could you be so certain then?'

Haril hesitated. What the girl said was true. He did not know how much pain he could suffer before doing anything Karn demanded.

'Very well,' he agreed. 'But first tell me – how did I get here? What happened?'

'Our people were watching from the forest as you brought Zia across the plain,' the old woman explained. 'When you were wounded and fell to the ground, Karn's men ran forward and would have killed you. Our people came to you first.'

'Then there was a fight?'

'No. Karn and his men fled when they saw us.'

Haril grinned. 'They thought you were devil-people.'

'That has always been our protection. Your people feared the forest and all that dwells in it. They left us in peace.'

'Then why do you worry about Karn? They will still fear you.'

The old woman shook her head sadly. 'Not for long. They have met us face to face now. When they took Zia and her brother, they understood for the first time that we are human like themselves and can suffer and die. They will gather their courage and come into the forest, seeking to kill us.'

Haril considered her words. Karn would want revenge, certainly. But uppermost in his mind was the question that had been puzzling him all along. He turned to the old woman. 'There is something I would ask of you,' he began hesitantly.

'Yes?'

'I don't understand. Who are you? Where do you come from?'

She looked at him for a long time without speaking. Then at last, she said: 'We lived in this land long before your people came.'

Haril stared at her unbelievingly. 'We have always been here.'

'No.' She shook her head. 'Even we were not the first. And there was a time when no people lived in the land.'

'No people?' The idea was so enormous that he couldn't take it in at first. 'That's not possible.'

'Long ago, there was a great cold. Even in summer, the rocks were frozen.' Her eyes half closed and it was as if she could see back to the time of which she spoke. 'The people of those days disappeared. In their place roamed strange beasts.'

'Where did the people go?'

'They were driven to look for land where the sun was warm. Whether they found it, I do not know. But those who remained were killed by the cold.'

'And then?' Haril prompted.

'Then the cold departed and green forest covered much of the land like a mantle. And our people came.'

'Where from?'

Her eyes opened and she looked at him as if she would see into his very soul. 'That I cannot tell you,' she said. 'I speak with you because you have travelled and have a greater understanding than most of your people. But there are things for which the words do not even exist in your tongue.'

There was no sound in the cave except the old woman's thin voice and an occasional crackle from the fire. Haril knew instinctively that what she said was true and he felt strangely excited by this new knowledge, as if it stirred a memory, not in his mind but in his very being.

'In the beginning,' she continued, 'we lived on the plains and hunted as you do now.'

'The pictures on the roof,' Haril breathed.

'You saw them? Yes. Our hunters believed that to make pictures of the animals they hunted gave men power over them.'

'And did it?'

'Perhaps. But also they enjoyed making beauty from the things of nature they saw around them, to remember in the long winter months.'

'Some of the shapes I do not understand.'

'It was a long time ago,' the old woman murmured. 'We do not know ourselves. Much of our knowledge was lost when others came who were stronger and fiercer than we and drove us from our lands.'

'Who were they?' Haril asked.

'Your people,' she said, and for a moment her eyes glinted hard like granite. 'Many of us perished. Some were made slaves, some even joined with the invaders. The few that were left had nowhere to go but the forest. Slowly, over many lifetimes, we learned to make the forest our home. And your people learned new ways also and forgot we were here.'

'You have reason to hate us.' Haril muttered.

'We do not hate you. It is the way of things.' She shrugged. The momentary harshness had left her voice. 'Even now, there are others who will in turn drive you from your lands.'

Haril remembered the strange, helmeted warriors he had seen on his travels and his anger rose at the thought of such people invading his village. 'We will fight them,' he asserted gruffly.

'Yes. It is in the nature of your people to fight.'

'But surely, so it is with all men.'

'No.' She shook her head. 'It is not in our nature.'

'Then your people are cowards,' Haril burst out before he could stop himself.

The old woman gave him a faintly mocking smile and he immediately regretted what he had said.

'You may be right, but such a word does not exist in our tongue.'

'I mean no insult,' he mumbled.

'It is our purpose to survive.'

'Why?'

'To keep a knowledge of things long past and forgotten. The ways of the earth and the sun and the stars that are known to very few but us. Because the time will come when it is needed. Just why or when, we do not know. Only that we must survive until that time.'

'What are these things?' Haril demanded.

The old woman laughed softly and turned to the girl. 'Our friend would try to fill one small sack with a forest of acorns,' she said. 'He would learn what his mind cannot begin to understand.'

Haril felt the blood rise to his cheeks. 'I'm not stupid.'

'And neither is a sheep amongst other sheep.'

Again the old woman chuckled to herself. But to Haril's surprise, the girl turned to her with a look of reproof. 'That's not kind,' she said sharply. Then, to Haril, she said in a gentler voice, 'Mogan has told me that knowledge must be found and not given.'

The old woman nodded and smiled at Zia. 'You have learned well. I am sure our guest will forgive an old woman whose days are numbered.'

As Haril looked at them both, the one old and wizened, the other young, smooth-skinned, and even beautiful, he realised with sudden surprise, he felt clumsy and ignorant in a way he had never known before.

'You speak the truth,' he said. 'But truly, I would seek to learn.'

'That is good.' The old woman sighed as if she were suddenly very tired. 'The seeking is all that matters.'

'Is it not possible for our two peoples to join together against the invader?' Haril persisted.

'No. Because after them, there will be more invaders. Through time, men will fight for this land and the rivers will run red. And we will hide in the deep forest and in the mountains and again men will forget we are there. Or believe we are spirits as do many of your people. But for as long as the forest is here, we will remain.'

Haril smiled. 'Then you have nothing to fear. The forest will always be here.'

She turned away, but not before Haril had glimpsed a great sadness in her eyes. 'One by one, the trees will fall under the axes of man until none are left.' Her voice was scarcely louder than the stirring of a breeze in the heather. 'The world will be an empty desert where the winds howl fiercely, for there will be nothing to tame them. There will be no shelter for us or for the wild creatures of the forest and then truly, at last, we shall be no more.

Or perhaps, that will be the time when our knowledge is needed. I do not know ...'

Her voice faded away and there was a long silence. Haril could understand nothing of the strange future she spoke of, but an icy hand seemed to grip his heart. There was a slight movement beside him. He turned and the girl was very close to him and holding out the cup. He hesitated, then took it and drank quickly. The liquid ran bitterly down his throat and almost at once, a gentle lethargy began to seep through his limbs. He looked up at Zia and their eyes met and held.

'Shall we meet again?' he whispered.

'Mogan has taught me that nothing is impossible.'

Haril looked round towards the old woman. She had returned silently to the fire and was now sitting beside it and staring into the flames and he knew her thoughts were far away. He turned back to Zia, who was smiling at him. She held in her hand a thin cord made of tree-fibres, attached to some small object that glittered. He was too tired even to look down at it as she slipped the necklet over his head. A heavy numbness was stealing over his body.

'Remember me,' she murmured softly.

Chapter Four

Birds sang noisily in the branches over his head. The sun shone so brightly against his eyelids that, on waking, Haril had to turn his head away and blink rapidly until he became accustomed to the light. He was lying in soft undergrowth at the edge of the forest, dank with the smell of earth and rotting leaves. Beyond the trees was flat, open country. There was something familiar about the hump-backed hills in the far distance.

He staggered unsteadily to his feet. The strength had partly returned to his body, but he was still exhausted and had a curious hazy feeling in his head. He reached up to stretch his arms, and felt something cold against his chest. Then he remembered the girl Zia putting an object round his neck, just as he was falling asleep that last time. He took it out and held it in his hand. It looked like bronze and was shaped somewhat like a leaf with an uneven edge. Haril guessed it to be a lucky talisman. It was shiny and pleasantly smooth to touch, lighter than he expected but then Haril had seldom handled bronze for it was usually owned only by the most powerful warriors and hunters. As he examined it more closely he saw some peculiar marks scratched on its surface, but they made no sense to him. He wished he had been able to give Zia something in return. One of his flints, for instance. He reached into the pouch of his leather jerkin and found that the few he had brought with him from Karn's village were still there.

He glanced back at the forest. The trees towered over dark, thickly tangled undergrowth. Nothing stirred in the gloomy silence but Haril felt that unseen eyes were watching him, making certain perhaps that he did not try to find his way back into the forest. He shivered and turned to walk cautiously towards the open country beyond the trees.

The ground before him sloped gently down to a wide valley and a river which wound its way across open heath. Beyond, a succession of low ridges piled one on top of the other until they rose to the high hills in the distance, blurred and shimmering in a summer haze. Wisps of cloud drifted across the clear blue sky. A hawk hung motionless in the air, waiting to pounce on an unsuspecting victim, and the thought came to Haril that Karn and his hunters would also be out there somewhere waiting for him.

He considered his situation. The first thing he needed was a weapon. It would take several days to cross the plain and he would have to hunt for food as well as protect himself if necessary. He fingered the flints carefully and selected one that was polished evenly on both sides and also had a sharp point; it would make a good spear. At the edge of the forest stood a cluster of saplings, striving for light out of reach of the great trees. Using another of the flints as an axe he cut one down and stripped it into a length of about his own height. Then he shredded some bark fibres from one of the trees and bound the flint tightly to the shaft. So intent was he on this task that he did not hear the sight movement in the undergrowth behind him. Too late he saw a glint of light dance across the ground by his feet. He spun round, clutching the half-completed spear, but knowing with a sinking heart that he would have little chance of using it.

The man who stood a few paces from him was holding a large bronze sword, raised in the air in a position to strike down across his shoulders. It was the reflection of sun from the gleaming metal that had warned Haril of the man's presence. He was an old man but his shoulders were broad and he stood tall and straight. He wore a leather cap with flaps that came over his ears and a brown jerkin similar to Haril's. His beard was almost white, in sharp contrast to the deep leathery tan of his skin. He had a large nose, bushy eyebrows, and wide-set eyes that showed strength and determination as they held Haril's stare. But there was no hatred in them and even as Haril waited for the expected blow, prepared instinctively to duck aside but knowing it would merely be a forlorn gesture, the man smiled.

The wrinkles about his eyes deepened. He looked like someone who smiled often.

'I will not strike if you put down your spear,' he said in a deep voice. Although the words were those of Haril's people, there was a strange lilt in them that Haril had never heard before.

'And make it easier for you,' Haril replied, gripping his spear and edging the point towards the stranger.

'I wish you no harm, my friend. See?' The man lowered his sword and now Haril had the advantage. For a moment, so tense had he been at the thought of Karn, he almost thrust the spear forward. But then he noticed the pack across the stranger's shoulders and the way he was dressed. And as Haril looked more intently at his features, he had a distinct impression it was a face he had seen before. But he could not remember when or where.

'Who are you?' he demanded.

'My name is Brond.'

'You are also a traveller?'

'Yes. I am a worker of bronze.'

The man glanced to one side and Haril saw, some distance away, a small two-wheeled cart which contained a crucible, lumps of copper and tin and other implements of the bronzesmith's trade.

'I didn't hear you come,' Haril said, putting aside his spear.

'If I had been an enemy, you would have felt only the pain of death.' The old man seemed to be reproving Haril for his carelessness. 'That's why I raised my sword. There are many these days who strike first before they know who they would kill.'

Haril flushed, knowing the old man was right, and went through the formality of introducing himself.

'Finish the spear you are making,' the old man said, 'and then we will talk.'

Haril hesitated, then bent down to complete his task. As he worked, Brond watched him critically. When the spear was finished, he nodded.

'It will do.'

'It's a good spear,' Haril insisted.

'Considering it's only stone.'

It was an old argument between bronze and stone workers, which was the better material.

'You cannot build houses with bronze,' Haril retorted.

'Or make a sword with stone,' Brond replied with a good natured smile. 'Come, we will not argue. Each has its own use. What are you doing at the edge of the forest? It is not often our people venture so near.'

Haril was about to tell him of the forest people when suddenly he remembered where he had seen the old man before. His face had been one of those looking at him when he woke from his drugged sleep in the forest.

'I think you know very well, old man,' he said accusingly.

For a long moment Brond stood there watching him. Then he nodded. 'Yes. I was there. I wanted to see if you would remember.'

Haril looked at him suspiciously. 'And what has a worker of bronze to do with the forest people?'

'Sometimes I trade with them,' Brond said simply. 'I happened to be there when they brought you in, and stayed until you recovered. That is all.'

Haril had a strong feeling that was not all by any means.

'I did not even know they existed. And now I find our people trade with them.'

'Only very few.'

'Even so ...'

'There are many things you do not know, my young friend.'

'I have travelled more than most,' Haril said indignantly.

Brond lifted his shaggy head and laughed loudly. 'Aye, to the mountains of the north. I know. Such a long journey.'

'Have you travelled further?'

'Yes. Maybe I'll tell you sometime.'

'And who are the forest people?'

Brond laughed again. 'Did Mogan not tell you that such knowledge must be learned by yourself?'

'Yes, but ...'

'I know little more than you. There, I am only a poor worker of bronze. And this pack is heavy.'

Brond swung the pack from his shoulders, placed it carefully on the ground, and sat on a tree stump.

'Where are you from?' Haril persisted.

'Truly, you are a great asker of questions,' Brond said, wiping the sweat from his brow.

'Isn't that one way to seek knowledge?'

'How would you know the answer to be true or not?'

Haril thought: Karn's people asked such questions of me and were not prepared to believe my answers because they were far beyond their understanding.

Brond was peering at him closely. 'This I will tell you,' he said, 'although I would not tell many. I come from a land that lies beyond the water.'

'I know there is such a place,' Haril said airily, trying to show he was not really impressed. But he felt his heart beat faster.

Brond reached into the pack and took out a lump of copper that shone a dull red. 'My country is where this comes from.'

Haril took the metal and looked at it curiously. He had seen copper before, but only very rarely. As he held it in his hands, feeling its weight, the thought occurred to him to show Brond the talisman that Zia had given him. But he decided against it. He felt instinctively he could trust the old man but his recent experiences had made him cautious.

'And now it is my turn to ask a question,' Brond said with a smile. 'Where do you go now?'

'Home to my village, on the other side of the hills,' Haril replied.

Brond looked across the plain and nodded. 'I go that way myself. If you'll permit it, I will travel with you.'

'I shall be honoured,' Haril said. And indeed, it was an honour. Bronzesmiths such as Brond were the elite of craftsmen, much as workers in stone might hate to admit it. Even Haril, in the few years he had been travelling, had become aware of the gradual change taking place as people turned from stone to bronze, if they had the means of paying for the metal and the knowledge of its existence.

Brond stood up and Haril noted that, despite his age, he moved with an effortless ease. He also had considerable strength as Haril felt when he clapped a bear-like arm across his shoulders. 'We will walk a while and then hunt for food. There is good hunting in the valley.'

Haril frowned. 'I had thought of going round behind the ridge.'

'Are you worried about Karn?'

'I'm not afraid, if that's what you mean,' Haril said hotly.

'Of course not, my friend. But he and his men are a long way from here. That's why I left the forest, to find out where they are.'

'You show me much kindness,' Haril said. 'Why?'

Brond was looking across the plain with distant thoughts in his eyes. 'I remember a young man such as yourself,' he said slowly. 'Perhaps that is why I wish to help you.'

'Your son?' Haril prompted after the old man had remained silent for a while.

'I have no sons. It is myself I remember, when I was your age.'

Brond turned abruptly, once more brisk and alert, and pointed across the valley. 'Come my friend. The sun is high. It is time we were on our way.'

'Where do you go?' Haril asked as they strode towards the bronzesmith's cart.

'Across the plain towards the morning sun. I have heard of a great henge of stone which is being built. They have need of craftsmen such as ourselves. But there's no hurry.'

'Maybe you'll rest in my village first.'

'Thank you. I have almost forgotten the feel of a straw bed and a roof against the rain.'

He picked up the handles of the cart and moved forward. The wheels made little sound as they rolled over the short, rabbit-cropped grass. Haril noted that the wooden axles were well greased with animal fat. He went to take the handles but Brond shook his head.

'It would be strange for me to walk alone.'

'Alone?'

'This old friend has been with me on many long journeys. My bones ache and my back is bent with his weight. But he is good company. Listen.'

The cart began to sway as Brond pushed it over the uneven ground. First came the sound of pots tinkling against each other. Then a deeper, echoing boom as the large crucible struck the wooden tripod on which it was hung. And finally a dull thud as lumps of metal rolled from side to side at the bottom of the cart. The sounds blended pleasantly in a rhythmic beat and it was not hard to imagine that, to a man travelling alone for many days, they indeed seemed to be talking to him.

And so began the journey to Haril's village. Sometimes the two men travelled in silence, each keeping company with his own thoughts. At other times they told each other of their travels. Haril quickly learned that his had been nothing in comparison with those of the older man and he was content for the most part to listen to Brond's adventures. A whole new world opened up to him, of other lands beyond the sea where people spoke in strange tongues and of wondrous animals and beasts whose forms defied imagination. From time to time they stopped to hunt, and although it was usually Haril's spear that did the killing, it was Brond and his deep knowledge of the ways of animals which showed the way. After a few days the weather changed and a storm blew across the heath so that when Haril held out his hand he could cup the wind like a ball. The rain lashed venomously against their leather jerkins, soaking them to the skin. But Haril was aware of little discomfort, so fascinated was he in what the old bronzesmith had to say. He learned that many of the superstitions of his youth were merely fears of the unknown, as he himself had begun to suspect from his own experiences, and that it was the responsibility, even the duty, of travellers to bring a wider knowledge to those people who remained huddled unquestioningly in their small communities.

When at last Haril recognised the hills of home, he almost felt disappointment, in spite of the anticipation of seeing his family and friends after so long. Brond seemed to sense this, for, as they climbed the last long hill which would give them a view down to the sea beyond, he stopped and turned to Haril.

'We have spoken of many things that I would not tell to others,' he said. 'You must be careful what you say to those who are not able to open their minds to the unknown.'

'I know that from Karn's people,' Haril replied with a slight shudder at the memory. They had seen no sign of Karn and his hunters, and indeed for most of the journey Haril had completely forgotten about them. 'But how then should such knowledge be shared with others?'

'By telling stories at the camp-fires,' Brond said. 'As you will hear me do so in your village, for they will no doubt wish me to speak. Make them seem to be merely stories of the mind, and then gradually people will be prepared to see the truth for themselves.'

'I will always be a traveller, like you,' Haril burst out. 'I will stay in my village for a while, then return to the mountains and go beyond them to other lands, as you have done.'

Brond sighed. 'It's a lonely life, without home or wife or children.'

'I don't care. I'll seek knowledge all my life.'

'Perhaps you will. If that's your fate. But remember, what is most important is to see with your own eyes and think with your own mind. Knowledge can be found in a blade of grass, or the flight of a bird. It is not always necessary to travel.'

'I will do so, all the same,' Haril said with determination.

Brond smiled and pointed up the hill. 'Now you must show me this village of yours.'

The full realisation that he was nearly home then came to Haril for the first time. He scrambled eagerly up the hill ahead of Brond, wanting the first view of the village and the women working in the fields, his mother and sister among them. How proud and glad they would be to see him.

At first, the village looked just as he remembered it, nestled in a green valley with high chalk cliffs beyond. Its very position at the edge of the sea and hidden by the hills inland had kept it remote and seldom visited by travellers. Haril felt a warm thrill as he looked around at many familiar landmarks of his boyhood. The stunted, wind-blown trees on top of the cliffs where he and his friends had dared each other who could go nearest to the edge; the trails though the chest-high grass where they would hunt for snakes and club them to death with sticks to bear proudly home for their fathers to present to the village elders, who used them for strange and wondrous potions; the meadow where he had first known the fumbling ecstatic pleasure of love-making, with a girl whose name he had forgotten but whose face would live with him always.

But as he looked closer, it seemed that something was not quite right with the scene before him. He had expected to see women in the fields and men watching over the cattle and sheep on higher ground. There were none. In fact, there was no sign of life at all. And there was something strange about the village itself. In his memory the peat roofs were straw-coloured and the mud and stone walls bleached white. Now, although it was too far away to see clearly, they looked a dull grey, with patches of black amongst them. Wisps of smoke spiralled up from some of the huts, but it did not look like the smoke of cooking fires. He was seized with a cold dread of something he could not even bring himself to name. He heard a movement beside him and turned to find Brond peering intently at the village. The old man's expression was grimmer than Haril had ever seen.

'We will go down,' Brond growled. He had left his cart several paces back.

They walked in silence down the hill, following the track that generations of shepherd boys had used. There were no crops in the fields outside the village. They had been burned, leaving the ground charred black. Dead animals lay scattered about in pools of congealed blood, carrion crows pecking at their entrails. The village had also been burned. Most of the huts were roofless and the walls crumpled. Every sign told a story that was only too familiar to both men: the village had been savagely raided, and not many days ago.

'It would be better not to enter,' Brond said softly, holding Haril's arm to restrain him.

'My family. I must know.'

'Let me go, then.'

'No. I must see for myself.'

Haril pulled away from the old man and walked forward like a man in a dream. There was no wall around the village – Thorin had always said that men who lived in peace needed no protection. The path ran straight through the fields and into the central compound. Before they had come to within twenty paces of the first huts, Brond quickly catching up with Haril and walking beside him, they smelled the sickly odour of burnt flesh. Apart from the dead animals they had seen no other bodies, but now there was no mistaking the terrible meaning of that smell. Not only had the huts been set on fire but the doors had been closed with the occupants inside. They had been burned alive as the flaming roofs collapsed, and it did not take much imagination to picture the dreadful scene as the victims screamed and clawed desperately to get out. Now only the ruins of stone walls remained, enclosing heaps of smouldering ashes.

Haril walked on unblinking, his mouth set in a hard straight line, trying to control the sickness that was bringing bile up from the pit of his stomach. Again Brond tried to persuade him to turn back, but Haril ignored him. One thought kept repeating itself in his mind. One word – Karn. He was responsible for all of this.

The home of Haril's family was on the other side of the compound. As the two men made their way through the destruction, Haril had a sudden glimpse of it between two smoking ruins. He stopped abruptly. Incredibly, it was one of the few huts that had not been burned. Its peat roof was still in place, the white stone walls unmarked. He ran forward, scarcely daring to hope. The wooden door was open, and if he shut his eyes to everything else about him, the hut was just as he had always remembered it. He stooped down and went inside. Brond tactfully remained several paces away from the doorway.

At first, it was difficult to see in the semi-darkness, after the strong light outside. Haril peered round the hut, blinking rapidly in an effort to make out the pale forms that lay sprawled about the floor in such curious angles. Even when he saw, he could not immediately take it into his mind. He just stood there, staring, shocked into a state of numbness. The figures were the naked bodies of all the young girls of the village. Blood had congealed on gaping wounds between their thighs and in the places where their breasts should have been. They had been raped and mutilated. From the agonised expressions on their faces, death had neither been quick nor easy. Several had even crawled a few paces towards the door before collapsing. Amongst these was Haril's sister, Sorin.

With a cry of anguish, Haril turned and staggered blindly from the hut, retching violently. He reached his arms out to Brond, who was running towards him. Then he fell to the ground and a merciful blackness came over him …

When he recovered consciousness, he was lying on soft grass some distance from the village. The sun was hot but there was a pleasant coolness on his forehead. He opened his eyes to find Brond bathing his face with water from a nearby stream. He sat up and looked towards the village. Several new fires had started. One came from Haril's hut.

'It was all I could do,' Brond said gently.

Haril remained silent, but reached out and gripped his arm. It could not have been easy for the old man to carry him such a way from the village.

'You will never forget,' Brond continued after a while, 'but in time, the pain will fade from your mind.'

'It was Karn,' Haril whispered.

Brond nodded. 'So it would seem. But it's strange.'

'Strange you call it?' Haril cried. 'Have you ever known a blacker evil?'

'That is not what I meant. You did not see perhaps. But there are no men among the dead bodies down there.'

'Your powers are great, old man, if you can tell from ashes which are men and which are women.'

Brond shrugged. 'One would think a few men might have been killed fighting. But a sudden attack at night? Who knows. It is better not to dwell on these things.'

Haril sprang to his feet, unable to remain still any longer.

'Karn will pay a hundred times for this,' he grated.

'What can you do? You are one against many.'

'I will die, but so will he.' Haril looked wildly around for his spear.

'Listen to me ...' Brond began.

'Do not try to stop me.'

'No, I would only give you advice.'

'It is revenge I seek, not an old man's words.'

'There is time for both.'

'And the time now is for death.'

'It will be your's, not Karn's,' Brond said. 'You will be killed before getting near him.'

Haril stared at Brond, almost with hatred in his eyes, but as the fever began to leave his mind he knew that what the old man said was true.

'I will gather men together,' he said.

'That's the only way. But you will need wealth with which to pay them.'

'I will get wealth, then.'

'Where?'

'You know so much, you tell me.'

Brond considered. 'There's one way I know.'

'How?'

'The building I told you of. Perhaps they have use for workers of stone and the means to pay them.'

'You're right,' Haril said eagerly. 'I'll go there.'

'We'll go together.'

'Come then, we must hurry.' Haril was impatient to get started. It might help to stop the nightmare pictures that kept coming into his mind. So intent was he on his own grief and hatred that he did not notice the weariness in Brond's body as he stood up.

'My feet will not hold you back,' he said gently.

Together they clambered up the hill towards the place where Brond had left his little cart. Only once, as they set out in the direction of the morning sun, did Haril take one last look at what was left of his village. But it was not as a sorrowful farewell to what had once been his home; it was to implant the memory of it deep inside him so that his fierce yearning for revenge would not weaken and his heart would be hardened for the task that lay ahead. He would never be satisfied until he had plunged his spear deep into Karn's body and felt his blood warm on his hands.

Chapter Five

Selem had a problem. He had faced many such problems during the years he had been working on the great project. Ever since he had taken the final, solemn vow, his life had seemed to consist of nothing but overcoming one apparently impossible problem after another. But this was without doubt the most difficult of all. It really did seem insurmountable this time, except that Vardon refused to accept the existence of such a concept. There was always a solution to be found, somehow. It was his fanatical drive that had brought them this far, against all odds. Lesser men would have given up long ago, as others had before them. But then, Vardon was no ordinary man.

The young priest sighed and stood up, gathering the folds of his long white cloak about him. He was slightly built and could just stand erect without his head touching the top of the animal-skin tent.

The man squatting on the floor looked up sympathetically at the worried frown that lined the priest's pale, ascetic face. 'That's the only way I can suggest, Selem,' he said. He was a short, sturdy man with broad shoulders and powerful muscles. He was naked to the waist and wore the traditional leather apron of a stone worker.

'It's dangerous,' Selem replied. 'One slip, and ...'

'I know. But what other choice do we have?'

Selem picked up the piece of parchment he had previously been studying. On it was drawn a series of designs, showing rectangular objects of various shapes and sizes. One section consisted of two large uprights with a smaller slab across the top. Selem looked at it for a moment, then turned decisively to the other man.

'Come, Gronik,' he said. 'We will see Vardon about this.'

The stone worker paled, but made no reply. He got to his feet and followed Selem from the tent.

The scene outside was one of intense activity. They were in the middle of a vast bowl-shaped plain, ringed by undulating hills. There were no trees, only smooth grassland. In the area where they stood there were many tents and some larger stone huts. Women were cooking over open fires, men scurried about like ants, naked except for loincloths, carrying logs of wood, tools, and large pieces of stone. The air was filled with the sound of workers chipping stone and hammering metal and the shouts of others giving orders. The camp covered so large an area that people on the far side were barely visible. Herds of cattle and sheep grazed in the sloping uplands beyond.

On a slight rise to one side of the camp was the centre of all this activity. At first it appeared to be a confused blur of movement, like bees swarming round a hive, as hundreds of men clambered over wooden frames and pulled at long ropes. But gradually, shapes became more distinct. A circle of stone pillars, the thickness of a tree and the height of several men, had been constructed around the outside, the distance across measuring a hundred paces. Inside this ring, larger blocks of stone were being erected, dwarfing everything else about them. As Selem and Gronik walked towards the site, these stones loomed higher until they towered over them, black and stark against a pale grey sky.

In spite of the years he had worked on the great Temple of Stone, Selem felt again that sense of wonderment as he gazed at the most incredible achievement of man. It seemed inconceivable that the stones, some weighing as much as a hundred men, could have been brought to this place, let alone cut to an exact size and lifted to the exact position required. And yet this had been done, over a slow, laborious period of time that extended back for more generations than anyone knew. In Selem's own time he had seen three of the huge monuments erected, and other stones were now lying flat on the ground, patiently being chipped and smoothed by dozens of workers. These were the blocks that had to be lifted on to the uprights to form archways. It was finding the means to do this that now presented Selem with his biggest problem of all.

In contrast to the work going on all around, the centre of the temple was a pool of stillness. It was guarded by a ring of Samothei warriors, fierce-looking men carrying bronze swords and spears, round studded shields, and wearing distinct red headcloths. Others could be seen all around the camp, urging the workers on with their tasks, lashing out with long leather whips. Some rode horses which had been caught in the distant hills and tamed, an inspiration of Vardon's so it was said.

One of the soldiers moved forward as Selem and Gronik approached. The workers around paused and watched curiously to see what happened.

'We would speak with Vardon,' Selem said in a clear, even voice.

'What is your business?' the soldier demanded.

'It's urgent, that's all you need to know.'

The soldier grunted, fingering the hilt of his sword. 'Vardon will see no one today.'

'He will, if he wishes the work to continue.'

For a moment the soldier stared aggressively at Selem. Then he turned on his heel and strode out of sight behind the ring of men and stones surrounding the central area. Selem waited, aware, not for the first time, of a guilty but mounting irritation at the way Vardon was treating even his own Samothei priests these days. Gronik stood several paces behind, pale with fear. After several moments, the soldier returned.

'You may go forward, Selem,' he said gruffly. 'But the worker will wait here.'

Selem glanced behind him and saw with wry amusement the immense relief that had transformed Gronik's expression.

The soldiers moved aside and Selem walked forward. Before him was an open clearing, in the centre of which was a long oblong stone that had been set in the ground like a table and polished until it shone like metal. It was a curious blue-grey colour. Only Vardon knew where it had been quarried. Several paces behind was a thin stone pillar, set perfectly upright, which marked the exact rising of the sun over the distant hills. To one side a large tent had been constructed, guarded by the biggest and fiercest of the warriors that Vardon had brought from other lands. He beckoned Selem forward. Selem stooped and entered the tent.

It was pleasantly cool inside, after the heat of the midday sun. Carpets of woven wool lay strewn over the ground and at the far end was a large couch, covered with silk furnishings and cushions. Two serving girls squatted on either side, one of them holding a jug of water. Vardon sat on the couch, staring intently at several sheets of parchment. He wore the white cloak of all Samothei priests but his was embroidered in gold with strange signs and his head-cloth was a rich purple. He had a long, narrow face, an aquiline nose with nostrils that were normally dilated but flared taut when he was angry, and a black, well-trimmed beard. But it was his eyes that were the most remarkable feature about him. They were large and black as night, glowing with some great inner power and conviction, before which even the strongest men quailed. As Selem bowed low to the ground, he felt those eyes turn towards him and they seemed to search into the deepest recesses of his being. Not without reason was it said that no man could speak an untruth before Vardon.

'I am your servant, Master,' Selem murmured.

'What do you want, Selem?' Vardon's voice seemed to come from deep inside him. Selem had heard it thundering so loudly across the plain that men were mesmerized and even the singing of birds was stilled. Now, with a chill running up his spine, Selem could detect an ominous note of annoyance. But he lifted his head, determined to speak his mind.

'The time has come to raise the high stones,' he said.

'And the time is late,' Vardon growled. 'The work is going too slowly.'

'The men are working as fast as they can, Master.'

Vardon stood up abruptly, strode to the opening of the tent and looked out. Then he turned to Selem.

'You know my will. The temple must be completed in my lifetime.'

'We are doing all that is possible,' Selem replied.

'Possible?' Vardon's eyes narrowed. 'It will be done, that is all.'

'Yes, Master.'

'What problem do you have now?'

'How to raise the stones,' Selem answered. 'They are such a great weight.'

Vardon clenched his fists. 'You know the distance each one has been brought. Across many hills, along rivers, over fields. A journey of several lifetimes. And now you dare to tell me you cannot raise them in place?'

Selem felt the sweat stand out on his forehead but he strove to meet Vardon's eyes. 'Gronik has suggested a way. But it is not easy. If the stone should fall ...'

'Then Gronik will answer for it. What is this way?'

Selem showed him the parchment he had brought with him. It depicted the design Gronik had been working on for so many months. Vardon stared at it closely, then nodded. 'It must work,' he said.

'Then I will give the necessary orders.'

Selem bowed again and withdrew.

And so the work began of erecting a scaffold of timber around the first pair of upright stones. Above each the timbers met at a single point, like the tip of a triangle, and were joined across by the biggest and roundest log that could be found. This was greased with animal fat, then many ropes were thrown across and tied at one end to a wooden platform that had been built on the ground, against the side of the uprights. The stone slab that was to form the archway was rolled forward on logs and placed on the platform.

At last the morning came when all was ready. Hundreds of workers were assembled on the other side of the uprights, holding the loose ends of rope. Soldiers strode amongst them, whips ready to lash them into even greater effort. Vardon came out to watch the operation, flanked by Selem and the other Samothei priests. A soft wind stirred their white cloaks and cooled the sweat on the bodies of the workers. Gronik, who as the chief stone worker was in charge, stood with several of his assistants on top of the upright stones. The entire camp was gathered around to watch; women, children, soldiers, bronzesmiths, stone workers, hunters, even the shepherds who had come down from the hills. The whole world seemed to be watching, even the sun which had climbed over the sighting stone by the altar and now shone warmly from a blue sky.

From where he stood, high above the silent crowd, Gronik had a clear view on all sides over the vast plain. It had never looked more beautiful, the broad swathes of green grass, the heather and gorse alive with bees and bright butterflies, the river winding its way to the distant hills. He glanced up at the Sun-god, his eyes creased against the glare, a murmured prayer on his lips. Finally, he looked down at Vardon, a small but unmistakable figure far below him. Vardon nodded. Gronik bowed low, then turned to the workers who were holding the ropes and staring intently up at him.

Slowly, he lifted his arm. The workers pulled at the ropes until they were taut. For what seemed an eternity there was no sound, no movement, as everyone waited for his final signal. Once it was given, there was no going back. Gronik felt a momentary panic that his limbs had frozen and he was unable to move. He took a deep breath and quickly lowered his arm.

A great shout went up as the workers strained at the ropes and slowly, almost imperceptibly, the huge stone inched off the ground. The timbers groaned and creaked as they took the immense weight. But they held.

Gradually the stone rose higher on the wooden platform. Men ran to and fro below, pulling at ropes to keep the platform on an even level. The air was filled with shouts and curses. As the ropes strained over the log on top, biting into the wood, Gronik and his men rubbed on fat to keep them greased. Down below, the priests began a sonorous, chanting prayer. Small children leapt up and down with excitement, dodging cuffs when they happened to tread on their elders' feet.

Inch by inch the stone was pulled up the side of the great monuments. Putting those in place had been dramatic enough; they had been pulled upright with ropes and slipped into the foundation pits that had been dug to receive them. But this was the culmination of all that effort. It truly seemed that, at last, the end of the great project was in sight, a project that one way or another had occupied the lives of all those present and countless generations before them.

The sun was high in the sky by the time the great stone had been lifted half-way up. Some workers had collapsed under the strain. They were dragged away and their places taken by others. Once, one of the ropes suddenly snapped. The workers holding it fell in a writhing heap, the other end of the rope snaked back and crushed the legs of one of the men on the scaffold. The platform sagged to one side and for a sickening moment it seemed that the stone would slide off and crash to the ground. But with great coolness, Gronik managed to order the workers to lower the other end of the platform until it was balanced again. Another rope was attached and the operation continued.

At last the stone was lifted high enough for its underside to be level with the top of the uprights. Now began the most delicate task of all, to move it sideways until it was resting firmly in the grooves prepared. It was well into the afternoon and the shadows of the megaliths made dark shapes on the grass. Gronik was exhausted by now, both from physical effort and mental concentration. In other circumstances, he might have seen the flaw in his plan before it was too late. But so near was he to success that he was anxious to get the task finished as quickly as possible. The moment came when the workers at the ropes were no longer lifting the stone up from the ground but were pulling it horizontally across the top of the uprights. Until this point, its weight had been distributed evenly across the scaffolding of timbers. But now the timbers on one side were not only taking the entire weight of the stone but also the pressure of several hundred straining workers, while the timbers on the other side were actually being forced sideways. It only needed one timber to give way. And relentlessly, fatally, inevitably, one timber did break, with a quick, sudden crack.

For a fraction of time, the scaffolding remained in position while the broken timber dangled loosely from the ropes. Then the whole structure shuddered and swayed and finally collapsed like sticks splintering under a woodcutter's axe. The stone crashed down on the uprights. Even then it might have remained precariously balanced on top until a means had been found of moving it back into place.

But the weight of tangled scaffolding as it sagged to the ground, in addition to the exertions of some dazed workers who were still pulling at the ropes, was too much. Too late did Gronik scream at the men to let go. The great stone tipped slowly over the edge of the uprights, then with a thunderous roar that rolled and echoed far across the plain, crashed to the ground, splintering into a hundred fragments, cutting short the terrified cries of several workers who were crushed to a pulp beneath it.

A long, unbelieving silence followed, while the assembled crowd tried to take in what had happened. Vardon was the first to move. His face was white with rage as he raised his arm and pointed at Gronik. 'Take him,' he screamed.

The soldiers ran forward. Gronik stared at them, then with a despairing cry went to throw himself over the edge of the upright stone on which he was standing. But his assistants, fearing for their own lives, seized him before he could plunge to a quick death. He was bound with the ropes he himself had prepared and lowered to the ground. While Vardon strode forward, a terrible look in his eyes, one of the soldiers stood over Gronik with a raised sword. Vardon motioned him to put it away and glared at Gronik.

'Your death will not be that easy,' he snarled.

Selem had intended to plead for the stone worker's life or at least for a merciful death. But one look at Vardon's face and the words died on his lips.

Vardon moved forward and grimly surveyed the destruction before him. The stone that now lay shattered on the ground had taken years to quarry and bring to the site of the temple. There were others nearby, ready to be lifted on to the uprights. But the problem of how to do so still remained.

'What do you propose next, Selem?' Vardon said in a soft, menacing voice. Instinctively and fearfully, all those around drew back.

Selem felt a cold dread in the pit of his stomach. He tried to speak, but the words would not come.

'Well?' Vardon demanded.

'We – we will prepare another plan, Master,' Selem stammered.

Vardon laughed harshly. 'And will you stake your life on it this time?'

Selem stared at him. It was a basic rule of the priesthood that a priest's life was sacred. No one had the power to end it, not even the high priest. He could not believe even Vardon would do so. But then, many things had changed over the past few years. Vardon had become more withdrawn, more fanatical, crueller in every way as he drove the workers to the limit of their endurance. They had started as eager volunteers, willing to give of their best for little payment in order to complete the great Temple of Stone. Now they were treated as slaves, except for the key craftsmen whose skills were indispensable.

'My death would not help you,' Selem said quietly. 'And neither will Gronik's.'

'No?' Vardon looked across at the sun which now hung like a great orange disc over the rim of the hills. 'It has come to me that the temple requires a sacrifice.'

'We have animals prepared for the purpose,' Selem replied.

Vardon looked at him, a strange smile on his lips. 'Do you think that animals will satisfy the Sun-god?'

Selem frowned. 'I don't understand Master.'

'Since the altar stone was put in place, I have seen strange pictures in my mind,' Vardon murmured.

'The Sun-god has spoken to you?'

'Yes. He is not pleased with our sacrifices.'

'You are sure, Master?'

'You saw what happened today.'

Selem shuddered. 'But what more can we do?'

There was a long silence as Vardon continued to stare at the young priest. Selem shifted uneasily, aware of some sinister change that had come over the Master. One moment he had been more angry than Selem had ever seen him. Now it was almost as if he was pleased at some inner decision he had made.

It was at this point, just as Vardon was about to speak further, that a movement at the edge of the crowd distracted him. A group of soldiers on horseback rode forward, pushing the onlookers roughly out of the way.

'Who dares interrupt the high priest,' Selem cried.

One of the soldiers dismounted and knelt before Vardon.

Then he turned and signalled to the other soldiers. They pulled at ropes attached to their saddles. Two men staggered forward, bound by the other end of the ropes, covered with dust and bruises where they had fallen and been dragged along behind the horse.

'We found them travelling across the plain, Master,' said the soldier. 'What would you have us do with them?'

Vardon looked closely at the prisoners. One was young and fair-haired, the other old and grey. Haril and Brond had finally reached their destination.

Chapter Six

The initial terror and indignation that Haril and Brond had felt at their capture by the strange warriors on horseback paled into insignificance as they neared the temple and had their first view of the great stones being erected in the middle of the plain. They stared incredulously at the megaliths, hardly able to believe their eyes. In spite of his exhaustion and the pain of his wounds, Haril was still staring when they were brought before Vardon. It seemed impossible that men could have constructed such a gigantic monument. But the proof was there all round him, in the way men were working on the stones and rolling them laboriously over the ground by means of long logs.

Vardon watched his astonishment, the same half-smile still on his lips. 'You wonder at our building,' he said.

'Never before have I seen such stone,' Haril cried. 'So hard and pure, without cracks that can open under the axe.'

Vardon raised his eyebrows. 'You know about such things?' he asked.

'I am a worker of stone.'

'So.' Vardon turned to Brond. 'And you also, old man?'

'I work with bronze,' Brond answered gruffly. 'And I am not accustomed to being treated in this way, like a criminal.'

'Be silent,' shouted the soldier. 'And bow your head before the high priest.'

He pushed Brond roughly from behind and sent him sprawling to the ground in front of Vardon. Haril was barely aware of what happened, so awed was he at the wonders around him. He bowed low towards Vardon. 'You are indeed a great priest to have built all this.'

'You have more respect than your companion,' Vardon said. 'I have need of craftsmen such as yourselves. You would work for me?'

'Yes,' Haril breathed. The chance of working on such a project sent the blood racing through his body. And it would also bring the day nearer when he could seek his revenge against Karn, which was never far from his thoughts.

'That is why we came,' Brond grumbled, struggling to his feet. 'Before your men attacked us.'

'I am sorry for their behaviour,' Vardon replied, signalling the soldiers to untie their bonds. 'But you are insolent, old man. Those who work for me must learn to guard their tongues.'

'Is that more important than work such as this?' Brond demanded, pointing contemptuously at the shattered stone on the ground beside Vardon. 'You do indeed need craftsmen.'

'Be quiet,' Haril whispered urgently, knowing Brond's fearless determination always to speak his mind. But it was too late. Vardon had heard the words. His brow darkened. He motioned the soldiers forward.

'It seems you must be taught a lesson,' he said coldly.

Haril stared desperately about him, seeking some way of helping Brond by distracting Vardon's attention.

'I can see how the stone fell,' he said quickly. And indeed, in the moments before Brond's outburst, he had been examining the broken scaffold.

'Silence,' Vardon commanded. Two of the soldiers had taken hold of Brond. Another was unwinding a vicious-looking whip.

'It was badly constructed,' Haril continued wildly. 'See, the weight was too great for one side alone.'

Vardon turned slowly towards Haril. 'And you know about such matters?' His voice was soft, ominously so to those who knew him and would have taken warning from it. But Haril did not know him.

'I told you I am a worker of stone,' he boasted.

'Of course. So. You could do better than the man who attempted to raise this stone.'

Too late did Haril see the trap he was falling in to. But there was no turning back now.

'Why, yes – I think so.'

'Then you will show me how.'

Haril thought quickly. 'But the stone is broken.'

'We have others here.'

'It will take time to make adjustments for the correct weights,' Haril said, trying to sound confident. 'It is not a simple matter.'

Vardon smiled grimly. 'You are right. So I will give you until tomorrow to prepare your plan.'

'Tomorrow?' Haril stared at the mighty stones, towering up over them until they seemed to reach the very sky. To lift another huge stone up to that height? 'But that is not possible.'

'I hope it is for your sake. Tonight you will taste the rewards that will be yours should you succeed. But if you do not, this night will be your last. For both of you.' Vardon turned to the soldiers. 'Take them away.'

Aghast at what he had done, Haril allowed himself to be led away by the soldiers. Brond walked beside him, saying nothing but occasionally darting curious glances at him from beneath his bushy eyebrows. They were taken past the tents of the main camp and eventually ushered into a large stone hut, comfortably furnished with carpets, straw beds, and a table on which were placed pitchers of water. Clean garments were laid out on the beds.

The soldiers withdrew but two of them remained on guard outside the door.

Stripping to the waist, Brond began washing the dust and sweat from his body. Haril sat dejectedly on one of the beds.

'So, my friend,' Brond said, splashing the water over his face, 'you have a plan.'

'If only that were so,' Haril groaned.

'Hah, I thought not.'

'I spoke too hastily.'

'And foolishly.'

'It saved you from a beating,' Haril retorted.

'That would have been better than death.'

Haril gently rubbed the bruises on his wrists where the ropes had bound him. 'Do you think he really means it?'

'Did you not see into his eyes?' Brond replied harshly. 'He means it.'

Haril sat in silence while Brond dried himself and selected a clean garment from those on the bed.

'It's the greatest building in the world,' Haril said, recalling the awe he had felt on first seeing the huge stones. 'They are truly a mighty people, these priests.'

Brond nodded. 'There's much we would have learned from them.'

'Is there nothing we can do?'

Brond walked to the doorway and looked outside. Darkness was falling and the first stars had appeared in the night sky. 'I am an old man,' he said slowly. 'Death would be no stranger to me. But you, my young friend?' He turned to Haril and smiled. 'Your time has not yet come.'

'The task is impossible,' Haril said gloomily. 'I don't see how anyone can raise the stones.'

'We will see.'

Haril stared at him. 'You know a way?'

'Perhaps. I must think about it.'

Brond lay down on one of the beds and stretched himself out, gazing up at the ceiling. Haril looked at him for a moment, then quietly washed and dressed himself. He had just finished when one of the soldiers entered, holding a lighted torch.

'Come, it is time to eat,' he said gruffly.

Haril glanced across the room at Brond.

'You go,' Brond said. 'I'll remain here.'

Haril hesitated, then shrugged and followed the soldier from the hut.

Some distance away there stood a very large tent, lighted by many flickering torches. As Haril came nearer, he could hear the sound of laughter and shouting. The soldier pulled back the opening and nodded for Haril to go inside.

In the middle of the tent was a long table, laden with great bowls of soup, joints of meat, and fruit such as Haril had never seen before. About thirty men were sitting on benches on either side, eating and drinking gustily. From the various garments they wore Haril recognised them as craftsmen, some stone workers such as himself and other workers in bronze and wood. There were no priests or soldiers present. At the head of the table stood an empty chair.

The men looked up as Haril entered. 'Welcome,' one of them cried, jumping to his feet and coming over to him. 'We have kept a place for you.'

He took Haril's arm and led him to the empty chair. The men grinned up at him, then continued with their eating and talking. In a daze, Haril sat down. A joint of sweet-smelling meat was pushed towards him, and he suddenly realised how hungry he was. He picked up a knife, sliced off a large chunk, and began eating ravenously. The man next to him, a young bronze worker from his appearance, handed him a cup filled with a pale golden liquid. It smelled sweetly of summer roses and honey. But when Haril took a long drink it burned his throat like fire and brought tears to his eyes. He fell into a fit of coughing; a great roar of laughter went up and for a moment Haril thought he had been poisoned.

'Drink slowly, my friend,' the young man said kindly.

'It's not fit to drink,' Haril gasped.

'Wait. You'll see.'

Haril chewed on a piece of meat to take away the taste of the liquid. But after a while he felt a pleasant warmth stealing through his body and a lightness in his head. Gingerly he picked up the cup and took a sip. The liquid was indeed quite refreshing.

When he had finished, Haril looked round the table at his companions. They had also finished eating and were now drinking and laughing together. 'Are you all craftsmen?' Haril said, finding to his surprise that it was strangely difficult for his lips to make the words.

'We are the chief craftsmen,' the young bronze worker said proudly. 'Vardon could not complete his building without us.'

'Vardon?'

'The high priest. His hospitality is very generous to those he favours.'

'And I am honoured to be at the head of your table,' Haril replied. 'But have I not taken the place of someone else?'

Another loud laugh greeted his words. 'Gronik will not mind,' one of the men cried.

'He has other things to concern him,' said another, grinning at Haril. 'But you may be meeting him soon for yourself.'

Haril looked puzzled. He was just about to ask more of the man they spoke of when the opening of the tent was pulled back and a girl entered. She was scantily dressed in a short white tunic which revealed long slim legs and the swell of firm breasts. Dark hair fell about her shoulders and her young, smiling face was touched with red about her cheeks and lips and blue above her eyes. Haril stared at her, only vaguely aware that the men were shouting and banging the table with their cups. She was the most beautiful girl he had ever seen. Suddenly, to his amazement and the quick beating of his heart, he realised she was coming towards him, smiling seductively. She was followed into the tent by other girls dressed in a similar manner, who made their way round the table to join the assembled men. But Haril had eyes only for the dark girl. As she came nearer, he could smell a fragrance that was like spring flowers after rain. She slid on to his lap and he could feel her thighs soft and cool against his. Still smiling she picked up his cup, took a long drink, and handed it to him.

'We drink together,' she murmured.

Haril felt a happy singing in his head. Looking round the table he saw that the girls had paired off with the men. Some were laughing together, others had already coupled on the floor with straining, jerking movements.

The blood surged hotly to his loins. Reaching up he found that the dark girl's tunic had somehow slipped from her shoulders. His hands touched the smooth flesh of her back. She leaned forward and his lips felt the tautness of her nipples. Her fingers were finding their way gently and expertly about his body. He closed his eyes and gave himself to the ecstasy of her lovemaking.

*

It was already getting light when Haril made his way back to the hut, under the watchful eyes of the soldiers. Brond lay just as he had left him. He looked round as Haril entered.

'Have you been well entertained?' he asked with a grin.

Haril sank on to his bed. 'My head feels very strange,' he groaned.

'Too strange for thinking, no doubt. And it is nearly morning and time to see the high priest.'

The realisation came to Haril with a chilling shock. He sat up abruptly, ignoring the ache in his head. 'Have you found a way?' he demanded.

'It is as well I didn't join your revels,' Brond retorted. 'The noise alone kept me awake.'

'But have you?'

Brond eyed Haril suspiciously. 'Have you enough sense left to remember what I have to say?'

Haril nodded, ashamed. 'I hope so.'

'And I. Our lives depend on it. Unless you don't value yours as much this morning.'

'Tell me.'

Brond leaned forward. 'There may be a way of lifting the stones. I do not know if it will work. But this is what you must tell the high priest.'

Brond began talking in a low, urgent voice. Haril frowned, striving to concentrate and to keep a clear picture in his mind of what the old man said.

It was not long afterwards when the soldiers came. Brond was told to remain in the hut while Haril was taken to see the high priest. They exchanged one last look before Haril was pushed roughly outside.

Vardon was waiting under the great stones with Selem and the other priests. His eyes narrowed as Haril was brought forward. 'I am told you spent the night as if it would truly be your last,' he sneered.

'And I would know many more like it,' Haril replied evenly. 'Your hospitality is much to be desired.'

Vardon stared at him, surprised at his coolness. 'You will find my hospitality can take many forms,' he said. 'Tell me your plan.'

'I must use smaller stones to show you,' Haril replied. 'Perhaps your workers will help me.'

Vardon nodded. 'Order whatever you wish.'

At Haril's instruction, two blocks of stone were brought forward, each the height of a man's chest, and set into the ground to represent the large megaliths. Then Haril constructed a timber framework at each end, with a round log joining them over the top to take the lifting ropes. So closely did this resemble the former scaffolding that Vardon's brow darkened and a fearful hush came over the onlookers.

'If this is all you have to show me ...' Vardon began ominously.

'I have not yet finished,' Haril said. He was trying to appear confident, but in truth his heart was pounding and his hands were clammy with sweat.

The stone that was to be lifted was brought forward. But instead of constructing a platform on which to raise it, Haril ordered the ropes to be tied round the stone itself.

'That's not even as clever as Gronik's plan,' muttered someone in the crowd. Haril was uncomfortably aware that everyone else seemed to share the same thought. Pretending not to hear, he ordered a number of logs to be cut, slightly longer and wider than the stone, and squared at their ends. At last, all was ready. Following Haril's directions, a worker pulled at the ropes. As the stone lifted from the ground, Haril placed logs under either end so that they took its weight when he signalled the worker to slacken the ropes. Then he placed another two logs lengthwise on the bottom ones, forming a rectangle. The squared ends prevented them from rolling off. When the stone was lifted again, Haril put two more logs across these, then the same process was repeated. Gradually, a latticework of logs was formed under the stone as it was lifted higher, always taking its weight except when the ropes were being pulled. It was at such a moment that Haril sprang his surprise, knowing only too well what would happen if it did not work. As Vardon and the others leaned forward, watching with fascination, Haril suddenly picked up an axe and cut the ropes where they were stretched taut over the top log. The stone crashed down, but was then held by the framework that had been built underneath it. An excited murmur ran through the crowd.

'Even if the ropes break, it will not fall,' Haril explained. 'And the workers will also be able to rest after each pull.'

Vardon nodded, clearly impressed. 'But what happens when you bring the stone to the top? That is the most difficult time of all.'

Haril quickly built up the framework until the bottom of the stone was level with the uprights. Then he constructed a similar framework on the other side. Finally, he placed rounded logs on top of the whole structure. Taking the ropes, he gently tugged until the stone rolled into position.

'If it rolls too far, the timbers on the other side will still prevent it falling,' he said. 'And finally, we remove the logs from under the stone by burning them.'

He stood back, waiting breathlessly for Vardon's reaction, praying that the plan Brond had worked out so carefully would find favour with the high priest. There was a long silence as Vardon stared at the structure.

'It is a good plan,' he said at last. 'We will see if it works with the real stones.'

He turned and strode away without another word. Haril realised that he had only won a reprieve.

The work began that very day, with Haril working under Selem's direction. Not once during the laborious weeks that followed, as Haril's model was repeated in actuality, did Haril see the high priest again. Neither was he allowed to see Brond. Every night he was taken under guard to a small hut on the other side of the camp and food was brought to him. It was plain fare of the ordinary workers, and Haril had good cause to appreciate just how important were the privileges accorded to the chief craftsmen. He was always too exhausted to worry much about the lack of women, but he often dreamed of the dark girl he had met but once and whose name he discovered was Lileth. It was curious how unlike Zia she was, although both were dark-haired. His memories of the forest people were still very strong, but compared to the wonders he now saw all about him, as the great project continued, they seemed almost simple minded with their weird stories. Their world was a lifetime away, whereas Lileth, or rather the thought of her, awoke longing passions within him. But never did he forget his hatred of Karn or his burning desire for revenge.

Between Haril and Selem there sprang up not a friendship exactly, but a mutual liking and trust based on the work they were doing together. It was from the young priest that Haril learned something of the Samothei priesthood, how it was their duty to teach and to spread the art of healing and to mediate between the people and the great Sun-god who ruled over the world. Haril had only vaguely heard of the new religion before, but watching the sun each day on its progress across the sky, exactly marked by the position of the stone pillars, and listening to the chanted prayers of the priests, it seemed entirely natural and obvious. What more powerful force was there in the world? What being more mysterious and terrible? It deserved the magnificent temple now being built in its honour, with stones that had been brought from far away. Even Selem did not know how far; only Vardon knew where they were being quarried.

When at last the day came for the great stone to be rolled into place on top of the megaliths, it was almost an anti-climax. Everyone knew by now that the structure Haril had devised was fool proof although nobody except Haril knew it was really Brond's idea. It now had to be repeated with each of the other pairs of uprights, a back-breaking task that might take years. But it was still with a great sense of achievement that Haril watched the stone settle into place as the logs underneath it were burnt and turned to ash. His archway was the first to be completed. It would last for all time.

Selem came up and stood beside him. 'You have done well,' he said.

'I told Vardon my plan would succeed,' Haril boasted.

'Yes. And it is Vardon who demands to see you now.'

A cold prickling sensation crawled up Haril's spine. 'What does he want?' he whispered.

'Who knows the mind of the high priest.'

Haril made his way to the ring of soldiers guarding the centre of the temple and they stepped aside to let him through. Vardon was standing in front of the altar stone, looking up at the sun which was a white haze behind a cloudy sky. He turned as Haril approached. Haril bowed low before him.

'So your work is finished,' Vardon said evenly.

'Yes, Master.'

'I am pleased with what you have done.'

Haril sighed with relief. He had learned from others how unpredictable Vardon could be.

'You shall be rewarded,' Vardon continued. 'Have you any particular desire?'

The thought of Karn flashed into Haril's mind. All he needed to borrow was a troop of Vardon's warriors.

'Before you answer, hear my words,' Vardon said. 'I have watched you at your work. You are truly skilled and could be of great help to me here.'

'Thank you, Master,' Haril murmured.

'I have also taken a liking to you,' Vardon smiled. 'You are bold and not afraid to speak your thoughts. So many around me are merely sheep. That is why I give you the freedom to choose. Should you stay and work for me, you will have whatever riches and pleasures you wish. It may even be that eventually, you can join the priesthood.'

Haril gasped. Few men who were not born to the priesthood were ever invited to join.

'But more than anything else, you would be taking part in the greatest building ever achieved by man.' Vardon looked up at the huge stones, his eyes burning with some deep force within him. 'There is much I have not spoken to anyone else, even the other priests. But when the temple is completed, it will be the centre of the world. Men will come from many lands to worship here. You will have such power as few have ever dreamed possible.'

The high priest's words moved Haril deeply, even though he did not fully comprehend them. But what really seized his imagination was the thought of working with such magnificent stone, so hard and cold and pure.

'It would be a great challenge to work such stone.'

Vardon looked amused. 'You have the heart of a true craftsman.'

Haril was unaware of the irony intended. 'You do me great honour.'

'And you are young. You have time to learn.'

'What would you have me learn?'

'The meaning of power.'

Haril frowned. 'I don't understand.'

'It is no matter for now. Well, what do you say? Will you work for me?'

Haril took a deep breath. 'I would dearly like to stay, Master. To work such stone, to be part of such a project. But there's something else I must do.'

Vardon's brow darkened. 'What can be more important to you?' he demanded coldly.

Briefly, without mentioning the forest people for he sensed Vardon's impatience, Haril told him of the raid on his village and his belief that Karn was responsible.

'I have vowed to seek revenge against this man,' he concluded. 'And if you could lend me men and weapons …'

Vardon remained silent for a while and Haril felt his limbs shaking.

But when Vardon spoke, his voice was more gentle. 'I, also, have made a vow,' he said. 'To see the temple completed before I die.'

'That is your right, Master.'

'Work with me until the main structure is finished, and then I will give you all the men you need to put an end to this Karn.'

Haril hesitated. It was the most he could expect from Vardon, he saw that. Also, he feared Vardon's anger if he refused. But at the back of his mind there was a sense of relief that by his compromise, he would have a chance to work on the temple without dishonouring his vow.

Slowly, he nodded. 'It will be as you say, Master. I will stay.'

Vardon laid his hand gently on his shoulder. 'You will not regret your decision, my friend.'

Now that the decision was made, Haril thrilled at the prospect of what lay before him, to take part in the building of such a noble project. He looked up at the massive stones, reaching upwards as if they would support the sky itself. There was a sense of power about them, dwarfing the tiny figures who toiled in their shadows. For a fleeting moment he felt something akin to dread; they seemed almost to defy nature. But then he concentrated his thoughts on how he would carry out the work ahead. After all, magnificent though they were, they were only stones, fashioned by flesh and blood. And was he not the master of stone?

Chapter Seven

Haril was given a large, well-furnished tent of his own and the rank of chief stonemason that had previously been Gronik's. But his position among the other craftsmen in the camp, as they saw the favours granted to him by Vardon and the amount of time the two men spent together discussing the building, was far more important than Gronik's had ever been. As the man who had overcome one of the most difficult construction problems of all, Haril was treated with respect even by the priests.

To begin with, as Haril supervised the lifting of the other stones, he felt a sense of awkwardness at giving instructions to the ordinary workers and was deferential in his dealings with the craftsmen. But as the days passed, he found pleasure in command and in giving orders that no one dared disobey. His manner became imperious, even with Brond on occasion. The old bronzesmith had been assigned a senior position amongst the craftsmen but it was still subservient to Haril's. There were times when he had to ask Haril's permission to use a certain piece of equipment or employ workers for some specific task such as stoking the fires over which he was smelting copper and tin. Haril would demand to know the reason for such requests, then flush when the old man raised his bushy eyebrows and regarded him with a faintly ironic smile. Nothing was ever said between them of the fact that it was Brond's plan that had enabled the stones to be lifted.

Haril was grateful at first for Brond's tactful silence, then felt resentment and a growing sense of annoyance at the continual unspoken reminder that his success had been due to Brond. He told himself that it was his original intervention that had saved Brond from a beating or even worse, but the feeling of guilt remained. Finally, he found it easier to avoid Brond as much as possible.

One of the favours granted to Haril was the choice of a woman of his own. Without hesitation he chose Lileth. Her slender, warm body comforted his bed at night, her skills at the cooking fire provided him with the best of the meat that was brought in by the hunters. He discovered that she had been sold to the priests by her father, a farmer who had more children than cattle and wished to reverse the situation. She had been used with the other girls for the entertainment of the craftsmen. Strangely, this fact was not distasteful to Haril. It even excited him, and her gratitude at being taken away from the communal brothel was all the more endearing. She would watch him with loving eyes, attentive to his every need.

It was while she was preparing a meal for Haril one mid-morning that a shadow fell across the opening of the tent and Brond entered. Haril was seated at the table with Selem, working on some designs that Vardon wanted inscribed on the stones. He wore a fine robe similar to Selem's except that it was grey and not the white that only the priests were permitted to wear. He looked up at Brond with a start and rose to his feet. It had been some days since the two men had met.

'I don't wish to intrude,' Brond said gruffly.

'You are welcome,' Haril replied, smiling to cover his embarrassment. 'You are always welcome, you know that.'

Brond looked at him without speaking for a moment, then turned to Selem and greeted him with a curt nod. Selem glanced from one to the other of them and stood up. 'We'll finish the work later,' he told Haril.

Brond said: 'I only came to tell you the new stone is being brought in.'

The stone which was to complete the circle of megaliths had been expected for some days, after its transportation across country from the far distant quarries. Haril turned excitedly to Selem. 'We must see this.'

'Aye, you should,' Brond said and Haril was surprised at the note of grimness in his voice.

The three men left the tent and Brond led them past the temple towards the river. A large crowd had gathered to watch the arrival of the stone. It was the first to be brought in since Haril and Brond had come to the camp and Haril was intrigued to see how it was managed.

As the crowd of onlookers respectfully made way for them, Haril was puzzled at their silence. He had expected the usual shouts and excited comment that greeted any special event taking place in the camp. But this time the people were strangely subdued and he noticed they avoided his eyes when he looked at them, even some of the craftsmen he knew well. Then he saw the reason for their quietness.

The huge stone lay on a raft of thick timbers, by which means it had been floated down any convenient rivers during the journey, a quicker means of transportation than pulling over the ground. But this last stage had to be over ground, and uphill at that. Pulling at the enormous weight with ropes were several hundred men. Or what passed for men. They were naked except for ragged loincloths; their hair was long and matted with mud and the skin was drawn tightly over their emaciated bodies. Some were little more than moving skeletons. Their cheeks were hollowed grey, their eyes gaunt and despairing. The men in each line were shackled by their ankles. As they pulled at the ropes and the timbers grated with painful slowness over the ground, soldiers strode up and down the lines, flogging lacerated backs with their whips.

Punishment of lazy or careless workers was not unknown to Haril. He himself had several times ordered men to be beaten. But generally, the workers in the camp were fairly treated. They were provided with food and shelter and even paid with small bronze coins which could be exchanged amongst themselves for various goods.

This, however, was basest slavery.

'Now you can see the kind of monsters you are working for,' Brond growled.

Haril turned to Selem, a sickness welling up inside him. 'Why?' he whispered.

Selem looked away, a pained expression in his eyes. 'I have seen this before, when the stones are brought in,' he murmured. 'It is not pleasant.'

'But why is it like this?'

Selem shrugged. 'How else could they be brought here? Free men would never accept such back-breaking work.'

'So you make animals of them,' Brond said roughly.

'Vardon says that some sacrifice is needed for any great project. I don't like this any more than you. But he's right.'

'It would be better the temple was never built.'

Selem turned to Haril. 'Is that what you think, also?' he asked. 'If I tell you there is no other way?'

Haril stared at the scene of pain and misery before him. 'I don't know,' he whispered. 'I don't know.'

It took two more days for the stone to be dragged to the site of the temple. Haril learned that of the three hundred slaves who had begun the terrible journey over a year before, fewer than one hundred had survived. Several more died from wounds and exhaustion after reaching the camp. The rest were rounded up after a day's rest and herded away by the soldiers, back in the direction they had come from. A sigh of relief went up from those in the camp. They could get on with their work and forget the suffering they had seen.

Haril spent several agonised days of indecision. He avoided both Brond and Vardon, trying to come to terms with what he had witnessed. Finally, the stone itself won him over. It was still in a rough-cut state, requiring the work of skilled craftsmen to chip and smooth it to the exact shape required. But its qualities were readily apparent. It was harder than any stone Haril had ever seen, flawless, and with the same bluish tone that gave the altar its almost mystical appearance. Running his fingers over its surface, Haril felt a fierce longing to get to work. Was it not worth some sacrifice to produce such harsh beauty? And what could he do by himself? To leave the camp would be a meaningless gesture that would only deprive him of the chance to work on the great building.

Just how the temple came to be built seemed to be something of a puzzle. The workers and most of the craftsmen were content in the belief that it was a place in which to worship the Sun-god. The reason for the outside ring of pillars being placed where they were was explained by Selem and the other priests as marking the exact position of the god as he moved across the sky, in the form of the sun by day and the moon by night, so that the worshippers could always be in contact with him. But what aroused Haril's curiosity was the mystery of who had planned the temple in the first place and begun its construction. When he put the question to Vardon, the high priest merely shrugged.

'It has always been so,' he said. 'As far back as the Samothei priests can remember, there have been stones here, or at least the holes dug for them. We are merely completing the task.'

'But someone must have started it in the first place,' Haril insisted.

'It was probably the early priests of our sect.' Vardon seemed indifferent to the whole question. 'It does not matter. We have nearly finished, that is what is important. I will see the completion of the temple before I die so that when my spirit goes to join the god, he will be well pleased with my work. We will watch over the temple together.'

His eyes glowed with a dark passion. Haril shifted uneasily. 'That is why you drive the slaves so hard,' he said hesitantly.

'There is no other way. Besides, they will be rewarded for their efforts when they die. Is that not worth some small sacrifice?'

Haril looked away. 'If you say it is so, Master,' he murmured. 'You know more than ordinary men.'

'Yes, I do.' Vardon's voice was harsh and forbidding. 'The Sun-god speaks to me and me alone. Tomorrow he will stand over the middle of the temple and touch all the stones at the same time without making any shadows. This happens only once every year. Then you will see his power.'

'How?'

'Wait. You will see.'

Vardon smiled, then turned and walked away. Haril watched him until he disappeared from sight behind the central ring of megaliths. So daunting was the chief priest when one was close to him, with his tall lean figure and piercing eyes, that Haril was surprised at how small he looked beside the great stones.

The next day, the mid-day of summer, dawned with a clear sky. As the sun rose above the distant hills, its first rays struck the quartz pinnacle of the sighting stone, bursting into a dazzling star-shaped brightness. The stone's shadow fell dark and thin across the centre of the altar as if it would slice it in two. The shadow grew shorter as the sun climbed higher but never slanted to one side or the other as on other days.

There was an undercurrent of excitement in the camp. No one knew exactly what was to take place but as noon approached, a vast crowd began to collect round the temple. The soldiers were still standing guard so it was not possible to see through to the central area in which stood the altar. But as if drawn by a magnet, everyone seemed to know it was there that some momentous event would occur. It was whispered that no less than nineteen sheep were to be sacrificed, one for each of the pillars.

When the sun was nearly overhead, so that only small patches of shadow lay on the ground, the soldiers facing the crowd moved sideways to stand in front of the megaliths, thus giving a view through to the central area. The crowd pressed forward, straining to see what was happening. Haril, Brond, and other senior craftsmen were grouped in an advantageous position in front.

The priests, all wearing long white cloaks and headcloths, were standing on the other side of the megaliths, facing the altar. But it was on the imposing figure of Vardon that every eye was fixed. He stood between the sighting stone and the altar, dressed in his most splendid regalia of purple and embroidered gold. He stared at the crowd, motionless, and gradually all sounds ceased until there was utter silence. The he raised his right arm and pointed to a small tent that had been erected just outside the circle of megaliths. The opening was pulled back and two soldiers emerged, dragging a curious bundle behind them, so limp and broken that it took some while for the crowd to see what it was. And even longer for them to realise it was the body of Gronik, smashed and mutilated almost beyond recognition. His name was whispered through the crowd like a breeze sighing in the trees.

Haril had become accustomed to some terrible sights since his arrival at the camp. But this was the most fearful of all. It seemed that these remains of what had once been a man must be dead. But to his horror, as the soldiers dragged him to the altar, a strangled moan came from Gronik's torn lips.

The soldiers draped him across the altar. There was no need to tie him down; he could not have moved, with every bone in his body splintered. Only a spasmodic twitching of his flesh showed that he was still alive.

Vardon raised his arms high above his head. 'This is the man you once knew as Gronik,' he called out in a deep voice that rolled and echoed across the plain. 'And this is his punishment for failing the Sun-god. As the stone he lifted was broken, so is his body. But the mighty god of day and night demands one last sacrifice, so that he will look upon us with favour. If we do not do his will, he will strike the stones until they fall to the ground and crush all of us beneath them.'

The crowd groaned. Vardon lowered his arms and picked up a thin bronze knife which gleamed in the sunlight. It was one which Brond had made. He raised it over Gronik's body.

'What is your wish?' he cried out. 'Now is the time when there is no shadow. The Sun-god is with us. Do we obey his will or suffer his terrible vengeance?'

No one spoke at first. Then a single voice shouted, 'Kill him.' The cry was taken up by others until the stones shook with the roar. 'Kill, kill, kill ...' The sound pounded out in a rhythmic beat. Haril's mind suddenly went back to the scene in the quarry when Karn was about to kill Zia's brother. He was sickened at what he saw and felt no urge this time to join in the shouting, no blood-lust. But he could not take his eyes away. He stared fascinated as Vardon lifted the knife higher. Gronik's eyes fluttered open and his body began to tremble. Then Vardon brought the knife down in a sweeping arc and plunged it into Gronik's heart. Gronik gave one high-pitched scream. Blood spurted out from the wound and ran in a pulsating flood over the altar.

As quickly as it had started, the shouting died down. There was a long silence. Then the priests began chanting and moved forward to form a procession. Led by Vardon they moved slowly past the altar and away to their own part of the camp. When the last of them had gone, the soldiers regrouped around the central area. The altar and Gronik's body were hidden once more.

It was some time before the crowd began to drift away, each man with his own thoughts. Haril turned towards Brond. He wanted the reassurance of the old man's presence. But Brond was not there.

Not until evening did Haril see Brond again, although he had searched for him all through the camp. Brond was packing his tools and pieces of copper and tin into his little cart. He was taking nothing he had not brought with him.

'Where are you going?'

'Anywhere away from this place,' Brond replied gruffly. 'This is a place of evil.'

Haril sat on a stool outside the tent which Brond had been given. 'Don't you believe what Vardon said?'

'Do you?'

Haril stared down at the ground. 'I don't know.'

'This Sun-god the priests worship,' Brond went on. 'Maybe he is real, maybe he is not. But if he demands such a sacrifice, then he is evil too. I want no part in it.'

He put the last of his goods into the cart and turned to Haril. 'Come with me,' he said. 'We will travel where the air is fresh and men are not slaves.'

Haril took a long look round the camp. The evening fires were being lit. He could hear men and women talking together, now that the work of the day was done. They would eat and make love and sleep. They were at peace. The death of Gronik was already forgotten. It might never have happened.

'We will never again find such a place as this,' he murmured.

'It would be better if it did not exist.'

'How can you say that? Look at the stones. Are they not truly magnificent?'

They looked up at the temple, stark against the pale evening sky. 'The price they demand is too high,' Brond said.

'There's always a price.'

'That's Vardon speaking.'

'Perhaps he's right.'

'Then you won't come with me?'

Haril stood up and slowly shook his head. 'What men do may be evil. But the stones are not. They are true and pure. They will be here long after we are dead. I will never have the chance again to work with such stone.'

The two men regarded each other for a long time without speaking. Hot tears filled Haril's eyes; his throat ached with emotion. Brond reached and they grasped each other's arms.

'Goodbye, old friend,' Brond said in a husky voice. 'Remember some of what I have told you.'

Haril nodded, too upset to speak. The old man grasped the handles of his cart, gave Haril one last sad smile, and set off towards the open plain. His back seemed to be more stooped than Haril remembered from their last journey, his hair even whiter. The cheerful sound of the swaying crucible and the tinkle of pots and pans gradually faded away. Brond became smaller and smaller until he was a mere speck against the darkening shadows of night. Haril watched until long after he had disappeared completely.

Chapter Eight

As the days went by, although he still missed Brond's company, Haril became more and more immersed in the intricate cutting of the stones. He was proud to be part of such a great project in honour of the Sun-god, smugly satisfied in the respect shown to him because of his skills. Even Vardon showed appreciation of his work, treating him with a courtesy shown to few others. For the first time in his life, Haril came to know what it felt like to hold power, in the way other workers showed their deference towards him, made way for him as he strode amongst the stones, even the slight fear shown in their eyes in case they could not fulfil his orders exactly. The cruelties that went on around him were unfortunate, but as Vardon said, discipline was essential if the temple was to be built, and in any case the life of ordinary people was cheap.

It was only occasionally on some nights that Haril thought about all that had gone on before. The destruction of his village and killing of his family. Yes, he would have his revenge against Karn. But not yet. Building the temple was all important. Memories of Brond would bring a smile to his lips. He hoped the old man was well. But as he slipped into sleep, having satisfied his lust on the girl sleeping beside him, it was not Lileth's face that came into his consciousness but that of another, in a place of mystery where the sky was shrouded by the branches of high trees. A longing that he did not understand came over him, a longing for the girl who had caressed his brow, soothed away his pain, whose eyes brought a great sense of peace.

But there was no time for such memories by day. Haril was chipping a groove in one of the stones when a young man came up to him. It was one of the bronzesmiths he had met on his first night in the camp.

'What do you want?' Haril demanded impatiently. 'Can't you see I'm busy?'

'There's something you should see.'

Haril gave a grunt of annoyance but put down his tools and followed the young man towards the temple.

'Well – what's so important?'

The young man pointed to where a group of horsemen had gathered. 'It's Brond,' he said. 'They've brought him back.'

Haril stared, then ran as quickly as he could towards the soldiers, cursing Brond for allowing himself to be captured. Perhaps he could get him away somehow before Vardon was told.

But when Haril reached the stones Vardon was already standing there, looking down at Brond who had been bound with ropes and thrown to the ground. The little cart lay on its side nearby, its contents scattered in the mud.

'So, old man, you thought you would leave the camp without my permission,' Vardon was saying fiercely.

Brond gave a faint, ironical smile. 'Would you have allowed me to go?'

'No one may leave who is still useful to me.'

'I will never work for you again, Vardon,' Brond growled.

One of the soldiers kicked him hard in the stomach. He bent double in agony but made no sound. Haril winced.

'It is too late for that,' Vardon sneered. 'You could never work for the temple again, even if you wished. You are guilty of blasphemy against the Sun-god.'

At his words, those gathered round the temple whispered uneasily amongst themselves. Vardon turned to them. 'There is only one punishment for such a crime. Death.'

Haril stepped forward, intending to intercede for Brond. Vardon stared straight at him and there was a cold, deadly look in the high priest's eyes that chilled Haril's blood.

'Let no one seek mercy for this man,' Vardon warned, 'lest they be prepared to suffer with him.'

Haril realised the words were meant for him and remained silent. Vardon nodded, satisfied, and turned to the soldiers. 'Take him away. At sunrise tomorrow, the Sun-god will receive a new sacrifice.'

Haril watched helplessly as Brond was dragged away. For one fleeting moment, their eyes met. The old man shook his head, as if telling Haril not to interfere, that there was nothing he could do. Nevertheless, Haril pushed his way forward as Vardon strode back to the temple.

'I would speak with you, Master,' he called out.

Vardon turned, his face set in cruel, implacable lines. 'Not if it is about the bronze worker.'

'But ...'

'Be warned, Haril. I will forget he was once a friend of yours. But do not try my patience.'

Looking into Vardon's eyes, Haril knew he could expect no mercy, either for Brond or himself, if he made a plea for the old man's life. He bowed and turned away.

'Think of nothing but the stones,' Vardon called out. 'And the rich rewards you will receive. The time will soon come when you can seek out your enemy and destroy him.'

Haril stopped short in surprise that Vardon should remember his vow of revenge against Karn. He had almost forgotten about it himself under the sheer pressure of work on the temple. Now, as Haril walked slowly back to his tent, he faced a terrible choice. If he tried to rescue Brond and even if they succeeded in escaping, which was not very likely, he would have thrown away all chance of revenge against Karn. But if he did nothing, Brond would surely die the next day. It was an agonising decision to make.

Throughout that evening Haril struggled with the problem, sitting in his tent and speaking to no one, not even Lileth. His mind was tortured by the thought of the sufferings that Brond might be undergoing. Finally he could stand it no longer. He jumped to his feet and strode towards the doorway. Lileth looked up at him with a fearful expression in her eyes.

'Where are you going?' she whispered.

'I have work to do,' Haril replied gruffly.

'You go to help Brond.' She stood up and ran to him, putting her arms round his shoulders and holding him tight so he could feel the whole length of her body warm against his; her eyes were wet with tears. 'Do not go. There is nothing you can do.'

Haril pulled himself away. 'I must try,' he said gently.

'You will be killed.'

'Do not think that.'

'Yes, you will. You do not care about me.' She was crying now, with little animal sounds.

'I do care.' Haril reached forward and brushed the tears from her cheeks. 'You must go from here. Then you can tell them you did not know.'

'It is not my life I care about. Without you, I am dead.'

'Selem is our friend. He'll see that you come to no harm.'

'Take me with you,' she cried.

'I cannot. There's too much danger as it is.'

She stared at him, then turned away and stood there, a slight, huddled figure with trembling shoulders. 'Go then,' she whispered.

Haril looked at her for a long moment, then turned abruptly and left the tent.

It was dark outside and raining more heavily than ever. Mud lay thick and slippery on the churned-up ground. Very few people were about, other than the guards, and they were mostly huddled round fires, grumbling about the weather and the threatening storm. It was the rain and the rising wind that decided Haril that he had at least a chance of success, however small. As he made his way towards the hut where Brond was imprisoned, a plan was forming in his mind.

The prison hut stood some distance away from the main camp – so that the workers would not hear the prisoners' screams, it was said. To one side were tents where the soldiers were quartered and a corral for the horses. As Haril crept forward he saw three guards sitting round a fire outside the prison, under a shelter of animal skins stretched across wooden stakes. The rest of the men were in their tents, drinking and laughing with the women. Haril worked his way stealthily round the area until he could approach the corral from the other side. The horses were restive in the rain and moving in a bunch round and round the enclosure. Haril had never been so close to them alone before. Their powerful, muscular bodies, the stamping of their hooves on the ground, and the strong smell of animal sweat that came from them made him nervous. Most of the craftsmen and workers had never seen horses before and were afraid of them. It was one of the ways Vardon kept such a tight control on the camp. Great had been the panic one day when one of the horses bolted after throwing its rider; how much greater would be the panic, Haril reasoned, if all the horses suddenly ran wild.

Haril edged cautiously round the corral until he came to the opening, barred across by a long tree trunk. The guard, if indeed there was one on duty, was not visible. He was probably with his companions in the warmth of one of the tents. His heart beating loudly in his ears, Haril lifted one end of the trunk and carried it outwards, opening a wide gap in the fence. At first the horses were unaware of this and continued to mill round in the corral. Moving to the side nearest the prison, Haril picked up a handful of stones and began throwing them at the horses.

The first one to be hit in a tender part of his neck was a big black stallion, respected and feared by the soldiers for his unpredictable temper. He reared up on his hind legs with an angry snort that was taken up by the other horses. Seeing the opening in the fence the stallion galloped through; the others streamed out after him. In moments, the corral was empty. Haril crouched down, waiting to see what happened. He did not have long to wait. In the darkness, the leading horses stumbled through the ropes holding up one of the tents and brought it crashing down on the men inside. Their cries aroused other soldiers who came rushing out of their shelters with lighted torches to see what was wrong. At the sight of the flaming torches being brandished about, the horses panicked. They charged to and fro in all directions, knocking down tents and scattering fires. As the great beasts loomed out of the darkness, their panic spread to the men. A few of the braver ones tried to catch hold of the horses but most of them fled. In the time of a few heartbeats, the whole camp was in confusion.

Haril sped towards the prison. Two of the guards had already run away, leaving the third standing irresolutely at the entrance. Haril charged into him, clubbing him senseless to the ground with his fist, then picked up a spear that one of the others had left and ran into the hut.

A fire burned low in the middle of the room. Around the walls were bronze manacles and chains, set into the stone. Tied to one of these was Brond, his arms stretched high above his head so that he had to stand on tip-toe to prevent them taking the full weight of his body. His chest was bare and revealed ugly weals where he had been whipped. But, probably because of his age and Vardon's desire to keep him alive for the sacrifice, he had not been subjected to worse torture. He opened his eyes as Haril entered and stared at him in astonishment.

'What foolishness is this?' he whispered hoarsely, as Haril took the head of the spear and began sawing at the ropes that bound him.

'Save your strength,' Haril muttered, concentrating on his task. 'You'll need it if we are to get away from here.'

'You must have drunk too much wine if you think that it is possible,' Brond growled. 'Leave here now, before it is too late.'

'Be quiet old man. Did I ever tell you, you talk too much.'

Brond looked at him, half scowling, half smiling in exasperation and affection. But he remained silent.

It took all Haril's strength to cut through the thick, tough ropes binding Brond's wrists. When the first broke, Brond was unable to suppress a groan of pain as his arm sagged limply to his side. The second rope was now taking all his weight. It parted finally, with a snap, and Brond all but collapsed to the ground. Haril took his arms and eased him to a sitting position against the wall. While Brond slowly rubbed the muscles of his legs to bring the strength back to them, Haril glanced uneasily towards the doorway. The cries of the men outside could still be heard, but they were fainter and more distant now.

'Where are the guards?' Brond murmured, struggling to his feet.

'They have much work to do.' Haril grinned briefly. 'Can you walk?'

Brond moved a few paces across the room, weakly at first but steadily gaining his strength. 'I'll manage,' he answered, 'but I don't know how far you expect to go.'

'The Sun-god will decide,' Haril said, unconsciously repeating one of Vardon's favourite sayings. He went to the doorway and peered cautiously outside. The fire still blazed under the shelter but there was no one in sight other than the unconscious guard lying on the ground. From the sounds coming from the far end of the camp, there was still confusion as the soldiers tried to round up the horses.

'It's time we left this place,' Brond said softly, standing beside Haril.

Haril nodded. 'And this time I will come with you.'

The two men smiled at one another, then crept out into the stormy darkness.

Wind and rain howled across the plain. Thunder rumbled low overhead and in the glare from sudden flashes of lightening, the great stones showed as fantastic, ghostly-white shapes.

With their heads bent down against the lashing force of the rain, Haril and Brond made their way round the prison hut, past the empty corral, and on towards the plain. Luckily the horses had stampeded to the other side of the camp so that nothing now stood between the two men and freedom. They had all night before them in which to get as far away from the camp as possible, before Vardon sent his horsemen out to search for them. Brond explained, in short, muttered sentences, that he had not even tried to hide after his previous departure, which was why he had been caught so easily. Now they would make their way to the hills, remain hidden by day in caves or among the trees, and travel only by night. In that way they should avoid recapture until Vardon tired of looking for them.

Or so it seemed. They had not travelled far from the camp when Haril suddenly halted, peering ahead through the gloom.

'Why do you stop?' Brond demanded, turning towards him.

'I thought ... something ahead.'

'I see nothing.'

Haril creased his eyes and continued to stare ahead. He was sure something had caught his attention. It did not seem that anything was out there, and yet ... yes, there it was again. A pinprick of light, flickering in the storm. Brond had seen it too. He grasped Haril's arm and pointed to the left.

'This way,' he whispered urgently. 'We'll go round.'

But they had not taken more than a few steps when another light appeared. And another. To their horror, as they looked wildly around, they were surrounded by lights which began to draw steadily nearer. It was not long before they recognised them as torches, carried overhead by men dressed in chain mail, holding swords and spears. With sinking hearts they knew them to be Vardon's men. And there was the chief priest himself, striding towards them out of the night, the gathering light reflecting the angry expression on his face.

'I hoped you would heed my warning, Haril,' he shouted above the wind.

Haril shrugged. 'You know Brond is my friend.'

'A friend who will cost you your life.'

'So be it.'

As the soldiers came forward and seized them Brond spoke quietly to Vardon. 'Let the boy go. I do not plead for myself. But he has done you no harm.'

Vardon laughed contemptuously. 'I made certain he did not.'

'How did you know?' Haril asked.

'You should never trust a woman. Not after you have told her you are going to desert her.'

So Lileth had betrayed him ...

Vardon, who was watching Haril closely, gave another contemptuous laugh. 'Yes, you are a fool. And you have the weakness of all fools, to throw everything away for this old man.'

'Then forgive him,' Brond said quickly. 'There is nothing to be gained from killing a fool.'

'Only as a lesson to others,' Vardon replied. 'Fear is the hand-maiden of loyalty.'

'There are other ways.'

'But none of them as successful.'

At a signal from Vardon the other soldiers roughly bound Haril and Brond with their hands behind their backs. To the accompaniment of kicks and blows, the two men were driven back to the camp. Vardon watched them for a moment, his lips twisted into a thin, cruel smile. Then, gathering his cloak about him and bending his head down against the force of the storm, he strode towards his own quarters.

The fire inside the prison hut had been built up so there was more light than before, casting a flickering orange glow on the stone walls. The three guards were standing sheepishly by the entrance and Haril guessed they had been promised some severe punishment for allowing the prisoner to escape. This was also betrayed in the savage way in which they took hold of Brond and Haril and dragged them to the wall. Brond was tied as before but Haril was first made to stand on a low stool before his arms were bound to manacles over his head. The man Haril had clubbed spat in his face.

'It will be worth a beating to have you to myself this night,' he whispered. With an ugly grin, he gave the rope a final tug and kicked the stool away.

Pain flooded through Haril as his outstretched arms took the full weight of his body. It felt as if his shoulders would be pulled from their joints. The guard stood back and laughed.

'Well, master builder, now you know how the workers feel when they pull up the stones.'

'And you will know what it is like to be crushed beneath them,' Haril grated through clenched teeth. 'Vardon needs me to finish the temple. He will order my release and then you and I will meet again.'

A shadow of doubt crossed the guard's face. He glanced round at the two other guards who had been watching with amusement, but before he could say anything, another voice spoke from the doorway.

'We must learn to manage without you Haril.' It was Vardon. He had entered the hut with Selem and Lileth. The guards fell back with bowed heads to make way for them as they came towards Haril. Vardon's expression was cold and distant; only a tautening of the skin across his high cheekbones might have revealed his anger to those who knew him. Selem avoided Haril's eyes. Lileth on the other hand stared defiantly at Haril, her mouth set in a hard line. The desire for vengeance had driven all the beauty from her face, so that Haril felt almost pity for her. It must have shown in his expression for she flushed and clenched her fists angrily as she approached him.

'So you would leave me to a life of whoring,' she whispered venomously.

'To which you are well fitted,' Haril said with contempt. 'And by what you have done this night, you have the heart as well as the body of a whore.'

Lileth moved forward and struck him hard across the face with the flat of her hand. 'You will not speak so proudly when your skin feels the caress of the whip.'

Vardon was watching them. 'That smooth skin will feel more than a whip,' he said.

She turned to him abruptly. 'What do you mean?'

'Traitors deserve the cut of the knife.'

'But Selem said ...'

'Yes?'

'That you would not ... kill him.'

Vardon's eyes narrowed. 'Do you question my wishes?'

'I ... I mean no disrespect,' she faltered. 'But ... do you not need Haril to work for you?'

'The work will continue more slowly without Haril, but it will continue,' Vardon replied harshly. He turned to Haril. 'There is none so powerful that he can defy me. Just as I raised you from nothing, so I will cast you down again.'

Selem stepped forward. 'He tried only to save the life of his friend. And I did tell the woman his life would be spared. After all, if she had not told us ...'

'You think I did not guess he might make such an attempt?' Vardon sneered. 'I only hoped he would not. Now he must suffer for it.'

A moment of silence followed his words. Then Lileth threw back her head and gave a short laugh. 'Why not? What would it matter to me?'

Vardon smiled at Haril. 'You see what loyalty you command when there is no fear.'

Haril was biting his lips in order not to cry out from the pain of his tortured arms.

'It was ... fear for herself ... made her betray me,' he panted.

'That may be true. But she wished to see you flogged also. I can at least grant her that wish before the sun rises and you die on the altar.'

He turned and nodded at the guards. One of them strode forward and tore the tunic from Haril's chest while another picked up a thick leather whip. Haril closed his eyes, waiting for the sickening lash as the whip fell across the bare skin stretched tightly across his ribs. But suddenly, Vardon called out: 'Wait.'

Haril opened his eyes. Vardon was staring at the talisman Zia had given him and which hung from his neck.

'Where did you get that?' he whispered.

Haril was puzzled at the note of urgency that had come into the chief priest's voice. 'It's a charm,' he replied.

Vardon reached out, took it in his hand and with a quick movement he tore it from Haril's neck, breaking the thin thread. As he examined it closely, Haril saw that his hands were trembling and the blood had drained from his face.

'Where did you get it?' he repeated. 'Who gave it to you?'

'Why do you wish to know?'

'Answer me,' Vardon screamed, for once losing control of himself. Selem and the others stared at him, amazed at the outburst. It was in that moment Haril realised the talisman had some greater significance of which he was unaware. He knew instinctively that the forest people would be in danger if Vardon knew where it had come from.

'I don't remember,' he said.

'You lie.'

'Surely it is of no importance?'

'I will be the judge of that,' Vardon shouted. 'You have one last chance. Where did you get it?'

Haril shook his head. 'I told you, I don't remember.'

'We'll see.'

Vardon signalled to the guards. They knew their work well and needed no further instructions. Two of them picked up thick bronze rods and thrust them into the fire. The third tied Haril's legs apart so that he was now spread-eagled against the wall, unable to move. Then they ripped the rest of his clothes from him, revealing the white nakedness of his body.

Brond, who had not spoken since Vardon's arrival, turned to Haril.

'Have courage,' he murmured. 'You must not tell them. Remember that tomorrow, you die anyway.'

Before he could speak further the guard picked up a wooden club and struck it viciously across the old man's head. Brond sank limply against the ropes that held him.

The bronze implements gradually became hotter. Only when the ends glowed a dull red and were beginning to melt were they taken from the fire. The guards had leather pads on their hands so they could hold them without being burned.

They started on Haril's feet, moving the brands slowly across his skin. Haril cried out in agony. The pain was such as he would never have thought possible to bear without passing into unconsciousness. But the men knew the limits to which they could go. Whenever Haril's mind began to swim and a comforting blackness began to come over him they would pause in their work of torture until he revived.

Selem looked away, sickened at the sight. Lileth stared for a while, almost mesmerized, then turned to run from the hut. But Vardon roughly took hold of her and forced her head round so she was compelled to watch.

The stench of burnt flesh filled the room. The only sound, between Haril's screams, was the rasping sizzle of hot metal on a matted tangle of hair and skin. Ugly red-black weals grew about Haril's ankles and legs. Gradually they crept higher and Haril knew the time would come when the agony would reach his genitals.

'Tell them,' Lileth suddenly screamed. 'Tell them.'

Haril heard her voice as if from a far distance. He moved his lips but could make no sound. Somehow, he found the strength to shake his head.

'Then I will,' she cried, struggling from Vardon's grasp and turning wildly to face him.

'You know?' he asked quickly.

'He told me once as we lay together. But make them stop.'

The guards looked enquiringly at Vardon. He nodded and they stepped back from Haril.

'Lileth ... no,' Haril managed to gasp between bloodied lips.

'He got it from the forest people,' she cried, ignoring him. Her words came in a rush. 'Near the village of someone called Karn.'

Vardon stood motionless, watching her.

'It is true,' she pleaded. 'I did not understand his words but he did not lie to me.'

Vardon looked down at the talisman. 'Yes, he told you the truth,' he said slowly. 'Take him down.'

The guards cut the ropes binding Haril and lowered him to the ground. He lay there, almost insensible, while waves of pain racked his body. He vaguely heard Selem's voice.

'Why is it so important to know?'

'It is something only I understand,' Vardon said.

One of the guards moved forward. 'Shall we take them to the temple?' he asked, pointing to Haril and Brond.

Vardon thought for a moment, then shook his head. A change had come over him after Lileth's confession about the talisman. 'I may have a use for them, after all.'

'You want them to be kept here, Master?'

Vardon shook his head again. 'That would be too easy. There is no reason why they should not continue to work.'

'But they have defiled the temple,' Selem protested.

'I do not mean here. You go shortly to the mountains, Selem, where they quarry the stone.'

Selem nodded. 'It is a place I have never seen before.'

'Then you will take them with you. They shall know the real meaning of labour for the Sun-god.'

Selem went to the door of the hut and looked out. 'It is nearly dawn. I will tell the people there is to be no sacrifice.'

'They will expect it,' Vardon said. 'It would be a mistake to deny them.'

'But did you not say ...'

'Take the girl instead. She will satisfy their lust for blood.'

Lileth gave a cry and turned towards the door. But already the guards had taken hold of her.

'Haril,' she cried out desperately.

Haril groaned and looked at her as she was dragged from the hut. Their eyes met in one last fleeting glimpse.

'Forgive me,' she cried. And then she was gone. The hut was empty except for Brond, still unconscious, and one guard who remained standing in the doorway.

'Lileth,' Haril whispered through a sea of pain. Then he too slipped gently into unconsciousness. And he heard nothing of the terrible ceremony that was taking place outside.

Lileth was stripped naked and led to the altar stone by the priests. A great crowd had gathered in anticipation. Bowls of the golden liquid specially blended from herbs were passed among the people for them to drink.

Selem was waiting with the other robed priests and he also drank in his turn. As always, the pungent spirit burned his throat and brought a pleasantly hazy feeling to his head. But this time, there was a strange flavour in it that Selem had never tasted before. After a while, the colours around him seemed brighter and sharper, no longer dulled by the grey light of dawn. He felt that if he stretched out his arms he could reach to any distance, even touch the sky if he wanted to. The body of Lileth as she lay now, stretched out on the altar stone with her arms and legs apart and her firm breasts pointing upwards, seemed infinitely more desirable. The blood surged hotly through is veins.

At last Vardon appeared, a hawk-like, dominating figure in his magnificent robes. A stillness descended over the crowd. He turned his face in the direction from which the sun would shortly rise and lifted his arms.

'O mighty god of the Sun, ruler of the day, we are your servants,' he called out in a loud voice. 'It is to you we pray for the rain to feed our crops and the warmth to comfort our bodies. But there is another greater than you, and it is to him we dedicate this sacrifice.'

There was a surprised murmur from the crowd. Worker and priest alike looked at one another wonderingly. What were these strange words? Another god? Surely the Sun-god was all-powerful?

As if he understood their thoughts, Vardon continued: 'The Sun is god by day, but there is one who can strike him from the sky and that is the god of darkness. O Lord of the night and the dark spirit that is in us and all things, accept this sacrifice as you go to your rest.'

Selem looked uneasily towards the east. Vardon's words sounded suspiciously like blasphemy. But Vardon was the Master. Vardon was the one to whom the ancient secrets had been given. At that moment, the rim of the sun appeared over the distant hills. For a while it seemed to hang there, motionless; everyone stared, scarcely daring to breath. Suppose Vardon's words had given offence and the sun refused to rise? Even Vardon was apparently aware of such an enormity for he stopped speaking and stood transfixed as still as the stones about him.

And then, as if pulled by invisible cords, the sun rose above the hills and its rays struck the altar stone, bathing Lileth in its pure golden light. Vardon gave a cry of triumph, picked up the sacrificial knife, and plunged it into her heart. She gave one piercing scream as the blood flowed over her body, then her head fell back and she was dead. Vardon stood back and lifted his arms again, but this time towards the west and facing the crowd so all could see him.

'And now, you demons of the night, take the spirit of this your victim. Carry it away with black wings beating to that land where the Dark One is king.'

For a moment, all was quiet. Vardon lowered his arms and turned as if to depart. The people on the edge of the crowd began to move away. And then ...

No one was ever quite certain about what happened next. It might have been a cloud passing over the sun, but suddenly darkness fell over the temple. It might have been the bats which nested high in the archways but suddenly the air was filled with beating wings and black shadows fell over the altar stone. It might have been the liquid they had drunk that filled their minds with strange hallucinations, but as they all looked up at the darkened sky in trembling awe, each one thought he saw the thing he feared most. The shapes were barely visible and again could have been the effect of the sun behind dark clouds. But some saw phantoms of the animals which had once roamed the land. Wolves with snarling fangs and maddened eyes, reptiles with giant claws and bodies covered with horned scales, tigers with tusks protruding from their upper jaws. Others saw shapes too indistinct and horrible to describe, the beings of a fevered nightmare. Skeletons riding emaciated horses, with grinning skulls and hollow eyeless sockets which yet seemed to see. Birds with human faces and hands with taloned fingers, grasping misshapen bodies.

And looming up over the huge stones, like a grey mist writhing over some primeval marsh, were the head and shoulders of a goat. Its curved horns, shaggy mane and blazing eyes seemed to drain the life from all who looked into them.

Chapter Nine

Haril remembered very little of the journey to the quarries. At the outset he and Brond, their hands bound in front of them, were forced to walk behind the guards on horseback. Bur first Haril, because of his wounds, and then Brond, because of his age, could walk no further. When their legs gave way they fell to the ground and were dragged along by the ropes to the amusement of the guards. Eventually, when it was apparent that much more of this treatment would kill them, they were thrown into the little horse-drawn cart that carried provisions for the journey. There was little comfort as the cart jolted over the uneven ground but at least it gave them a chance to rest and recover from their exhaustion.

The journey took many days and for most of the time Haril lay in a semi-conscious fever. He was vaguely aware of Brond forcing him to eat and drink when they made camp each night. The faces of the six guards were blurred and indistinct. Only one stood out in his memory, the fierce bearded features of Gort, a huge broad-shouldered warrior who had previously been one of Vardon's personal bodyguard. He wore a bronze helmet and breastplate of which he was very proud, carefully polishing them every evening so that during the day they shone with a dazzling splendour.

Selem rode at the head of the group on a shaggy white horse. He seldom spoke and for most of the time he sat with his shoulders hunched forward, deep in thought.

Towards the end of the journey, as they slowly made their way upwards into the mountainous country, Haril recovered from his fever; he was still weak but was able to sit with Brond in the cart. Seeing this, one of the guards whispered to Gort. The giant stared at them, then shook his head.

'Let them ride,' he said gruffly. 'They'll need all their strength for later.'

Haril nodded gratefully. Travelling together as they were in a small group, some form of companionship had inevitably developed between the guards and their captives. Haril had once mended Gort's spear when the point broke during a hunting trip for fresh meat and Brond had told them stories of his travels when they sat round the camp fire at night. In spite of his gruff manner, Gort had shown some kindness towards them and Haril had seen something like pity in his eyes when he tied them up each night before sleeping. Only Selem remained aloof from them all, seldom speaking and always riding on his own some distance ahead. Haril had tried talking to him about the days when they worked together on the stones. But Selem barely answered and always kept his eyes averted from Haril's as if afraid of a direct contact between them. Only once had he shown any emotion, when Haril asked him about the death of Lileth. Selem became very pale.

'There are many things I do not understand,' he murmured.

'What does Vardon say?'

'The gods are pleased with our progress.'

'What kind of gods demand such sacrifices?'

'I do not know. But I have sworn to follow Vardon in all things.'

There was a long pause while Selem stared towards the distant horizon where the mountains were etched darkly against the pale blue-green of the evening sky.

'What's it like at the quarries?' Haril asked at last.

Selem frowned. 'This is the first time I have been there myself,' he said shortly. And with that he turned abruptly and strode away.

Several days later they reached the end of their journey. They had left the grass and forests of the plain and were climbing a rocky mountain path. All were on foot now. The cart and the horses had been left below, with one of the guards. Suddenly they were at the top, on a kind of plateau. It was very wide. Far across on the other side the mountain rose up in a sheer wall to become hidden in cloud. The higher they climbed, the colder it had become. Now a chill wind blew across the grey, desolate space, bringing with it a dampness that ate into their bones.

Gort led the way forward over the smooth slabs of granite. At first it seemed that the ground was flat all the way across. But nearing the centre they could see it was split by a wide gorge. In silence they stood at the edge and looked down. On three sides the cliff dropped almost straight down into a rock-strewn quarry; at the bottom, far below, they could see hundreds of tiny figures working at the face of one of the cliffs. On the fourth side of the floor the quarry sloped gradually upwards to the top. Clustered there were a number of stone huts. Fires burned in front of some of them and Haril recognised the men moving about as Vardon's guards. Gort nodded towards them and the little party set off in that direction, walking around the edge of the quarry. Now that they were near their destination, the guards had resumed their curt, unfriendly manner. They tied the hands of their captives and jostled them forward with blows and curses. Selem followed at the rear. Haril took one quick glance at him but his face was expressionless.

As they neared the huts, Haril could see there were women among the guards, some of them cooking at the fires, others carrying large burdens. A few had babies strapped to their backs. All of them had the same blank look in their eyes that Haril had seen among the slaves at the temple.

At the top of the slope that led down to the quarry stood a number of guards, their swords drawn. They greeted Gort boisterously as he approached. He made his way to the largest of the stone huts while the guards turned and stared curiously at Haril and Brond. From the hut there appeared a Druid priest; he was small and old, but there was a surprising lightness in his step as he walked forward. Selem went across to him and the two men spoke together while Gort stood respectfully to one side.

Haril felt Brond shivering beside him.

'This is not a good place,' Brond growled. 'The cold makes my bones ache.'

'It may be warmer down in the quarry,' Haril replied.

The old priest, accompanied by Selem, came up to them. His pale face was patterned with wrinkles and his bloodless lips were twisted into a bitter scowl. There was cruelty in his watery eyes.

'So you are Haril, the great builder of stones,' he sneered in a thin, rasping voice. 'We have heard of you even here.'

'And this is my reward for serving your master,' Haril cried, holding out his bound hands.

The old man chuckled but there was no humour in the sound. 'You will serve him yet,' he wheezed. 'Only there are no honours for you here. You will be treated no better than the other slaves.'

'I do not ask anything else.'

'Then you do not know what it is to work for Korth. But you will see.'

'You are Korth?'

The old man nodded. 'I have been here alone for many years,' he muttered bitterly. 'Left to grow old while others share the glory of building the temple. But where would they be without the stones that I cut for them. Eh? Tell me that.'

Haril shrugged. The old man glared at him, then an evil smile came over his face. 'But now at last they have sent someone to help me ...'

He signalled to the guards. Two of them strode forward and roughly seized Haril and Brond. They were dragged over to a large fire where a burly man wearing a leather apron was using a hammer of stone to beat a bronze cauldron into shape. He glanced up as the prisoners approached, then took from the fire four thick metal bands. Haril and Brond were pushed to the ground and the man began to hammer one band around each of their ankles. The metal was still hot and burned into their flesh until blood trickled down between their toes. Haril clenched his teeth at the pain but neither he nor Brond made any sound. When the bands were tightly fixed, the man joined a length of chain between each pair, just sufficient to allow the prisoners to take a short stride. Then Haril and Brond were pulled to their feet and the ropes cut from their hands.

Haril experimentally took a step forward. The weight of the chain and the sudden jerk as it tightened made him lose balance and he fell against Brond. Brond staggered but managed to push Haril upright again.

The man laughed. 'Your days of running are over,' he said. 'But you'd better learn to walk quickly, for your sake.'

Among those who had been watching was Gort. He came over to them and Haril could see a gleam of sympathy in his eyes.

'Just do the work that is asked of you and stay out of trouble,' he growled. 'There is nothing I can do for you now.'

'How long do we stay in this place?' Brond asked.

Gort stared at them, then turned away with a short laugh.

'No one has ever been known to leave ... alive.'

With his words ringing in their ears, Haril and Brond were led towards the quarry. After nearly falling over several times, they found they could move with quick shuffling steps. Each one brought a fierce pain as the metal bands pulled at their wounded ankles. It would be some time before they learned automatically to take steps which were just short enough to prevent the chain from snapping taut.

As the guards moved aside to let them through, they could see clearly down the long slope into the quarry. The surface was strewn with small rocks and rubble but in the centre a smooth path had been cleared. The reason for this was immediately apparent; some way below them two lines of slaves, dressed in nothing but ragged loincloths, were pulling at ropes to drag a huge slab of granite up the slope. Logs had been put under the stone to ease its progress; as each log rolled from behind, it was picked up again and brought round to the front. The movement forward was painfully slow. On either side guards lashed the straining backs of the slaves, shouting them on to greater effort. This was the start of the long, long journey to the Temple of Stone, over mountains, across rivers and plains. Now that he knew the length of that journey and the magnitude of the task, Haril marvelled that the building had advanced as far as it had. It must have been many lifetimes since it was started, many lifetimes of suffering.

Haril and Brond were pushed to one side of the path and a guard led them down. As they picked their way over the rubble, the walls of the quarry began to tower over them, smooth and straight. Haril saw that there was no way out of the quarry, other than up the slope which was the only place that had to be guarded. And he saw something else that made his stomach heave with sickening nausea. At intervals along the wall were the bodies of slaves, their arms and legs outstretched and tied to metal stakes hammered into the rock. Some were little more than skeletons, either dead or dying, their heads lolling forward, tongues black and swollen between their lips. At some of the stakes was the gruesome sight of human bones, bleached white against the black granite. At others were the men who had only recently been tied there, groaning as their arms took the full weight of their bodies.

One of these men slowly lifted his head as they passed by.

'Water, water,' he moaned thickly between cracked lips.

The guard strode over to him and struck him hard between the legs with the flat of his sword. The man cried out in agony, his body jerking grotesquely as he strained at the ropes.

The guard turned to Haril and Brond. 'Remember these if ever you think of trying to escape,' he said harshly.

Haril saw the veins stand out angrily on Brond's forehead. Knowing his old friend was about to speak his mind, Haril said quickly, 'This just means there are less men to work for you.'

'There are plenty more where they came from,' the guard sneered.

'Where did they come from?' Haril asked.

'Right here, most of them.'

'Here?'

'Why else do you think we keep women, fool? Most of these dogs were born here. And their fathers before them and their fathers before that, for as long as anyone can remember. They are born slaves and die slaves.'

It was just as well the guard turned away at that moment and did not see the look of hatred and contempt that came over Brond's face.

A little way further down they passed the slaves who were pulling up the stone. Their bodies were emaciated from lack of nourishment and scarred from many floggings. The stone itself was only rough-cut but Haril saw it had the hard blue quality that he had admired so much at the temple. If only he had known then what it cost to bring it from this hellish pit. He wondered who had been the first people to discover the existence of such stone.

At last they came to the bottom of the quarry. It was a large place but the walls rose up so high that only for a short time each day did it catch the rays of the sun. It was sheltered from the wind as Haril had imagined but there was a foul dampness that was even more chilling to the bones; water oozed from the sides of the rock, trickling across the muddy ground to disappear down cracks in the surface. It was as if the mountain had split open and this part had fallen down into the bowels of the earth. Everywhere there was the stench of sweat and human excrement.

The walls were streaked with horizontal lines which marked different strata of rock. Groups of slaves worked at the rock face, chipping with flint axes to cut away large oblong slabs. Where stones had been taken away or the rock had fallen, a number of large caves had been formed, providing the only means of shelter. There were a few meagre fires where women listlessly stirred cauldrons of greasy soup. Some had small children with them, but they were not playing together like all the children Haril had ever known. Everyone – man, woman and child – was working at some task or other. And striding amongst them, lashing out with whips and clubbing with swords, were overseers, chosen for their brute strength from among the slaves and all the more cruel in their determination to keep their privileged positions.

The guard beckoned to one of the overseers.

'Two more for you, Malik.'

The overseer strode forward. He was a squat man with immensely broad shoulders and long arms. His small eyes were almost hidden by bushy eyebrows and bloated red flesh. Malik never went short of food. Like the other overseers he wore a leather jerkin and leather straps round his arms. He prodded Haril and Brond with the butt of his whip.

'Good clothes for slaves,' he growled.

'They're special. Craftsmen I'm told, from the temple itself.'

Malik's eyebrows rose in surprise, then he laughed harshly. 'They'll work with the axe here and like it.'

The guard glanced around him, his nose wrinkled in disgust. 'The stench here gets worse,' he grunted. 'I'll leave them to you Malik.'

'Don't worry. I'll soon make workers out of them.'

The guard turned away and made his way back up the slope. Haril noticed that none of the guards stayed in the quarry. It was left to the slaves and their overseers.

Malik gave Haril another hard prod in the ribs. 'Hungry?'

Haril nodded. 'We haven't eaten since this morning.'

Malik laughed loudly. 'Then maybe you'll eat tomorrow night, if you work well. Come with me.'

He led them towards one of the groups working on the rock face. Each man was holding a piece of flint in one hand and clubbing at an oblong-shaped groove in the rock. With each blow, only a tiny fragment of the rock came loose. Haril could see that even to get this one pillar out would take many times of the moon. He knew the hardness of the rock and when he followed Malik's instructions and picked up a piece of flint from the ground, he could feel it was of poor quality.

'Craftsmen should work twice as fast as anyone else,' Malik mocked, pushing them up to the rock. 'Let me see.'

Haril lifted his arm to strike. As he did so, he caught a glimpse of the man next to him. He wore filthy rags like the rest of the slaves and the hair hung long and coarse about his face. But there was no mistaking that nose and those dark eyes. It was Karn.

For what seemed an eternity, Haril stared at this man whom he hated above all others. He didn't wonder why he was there. He didn't think at all. He didn't hear Malik shouting, or feel the whip cut across his shoulders. He just stared at Karn, aware only of his desire for revenge. Karn turned to face Haril, puzzled. The two men looked into each other's eyes. Karn's expression was dulled, stupid even, as if the months of enslavement had softened his brain. And then, suddenly, recognition came to him, and with it a wild look of fear.

With a cry, Haril leapt at him, clubbing at him with the flint. Karn moved just in time to avoid a crushing blow on his skull and Haril felt the stone sink into the flesh of his shoulder. He was vaguely aware of the whip striking again across his back and of hands grasping at him. He pulled away like a mad animal, seeking only to kill the man before him. He raised his arm again as Karn fell against the face of the rock. Then he felt a heavy blow on the back of his neck and his eyes seemed to explode with a blast of light. And then there was darkness as he sank unconscious to the ground.

Chapter Ten

From somewhere came the relentless sound of water dripping on stones. It was damp and cold. There was a slight rustling nearby and something furry brushed against his leg and he felt the prick of tiny claws.

Haril opened his eyes to find himself engulfed in darkness and pain. His head throbbed as if it would burst open and it felt as if the skin had been peeled from his back, leaving raw flesh which stung like a knife-wound with the slightest movement.

He was in one of the large caves, lying on straw which did little to soften the sharp-edged gravel beneath. As his eyes became more accustomed to the darkness he saw the dying embers of a fire just inside the mouth of the cave. A grey mist carpeted the ground outside and occasionally eddied into the cave, its ghostly fingers searching each nook and cranny. All around Haril lay the bodies of slaves, men and women alike. At first it seemed they were dead, so motionless were they, but then he became aware of harsh breathing and racking little coughs. They were sleeping from such exhaustion that their limbs were utterly still and merely twitched slightly when rats scurried over them.

A groan escaped his lips as he tried to sit up. There was a movement nearby and a figure loomed over him. Haril recognised the shaggy outline of Brond's head and shoulders.

'How do you feel?' Brond whispered anxiously.

Haril gasped as another surge of pain flooded through his body. Then he remembered and sat bolt upright with no feeling other than his anger and hatred for Karn.

'Where is he?'

Brond put his arm gently on Haril's shoulder. 'You must rest.'

Haril pushed him away and struggled to his feet. He swayed for a moment, his head swimming giddily. 'Karn ... I must find him.'

'Listen to me ...'

'Don't try to stop me, old man.'

'Karn did not raid your village.'

For a moment Haril did not understand the words. Then he gave a bitter laugh. 'You will not stop me that way.'

'It is true. Come – I will show you.'

Brond beckoned him towards the back of the cave. Haril hesitated, then followed. 'If this is some trick ...'

'There is someone here who knows you.'

They picked their way across the sleeping bodies. Haril saw that some of the men and women had paired off and lay in each other's arms. At the back of the cave the ground shelved upwards to form rough ledges. On one of these lay the figure of a young man. The rags he wore did little to cover his body which was deathly pale and emaciated; his eyes must have been open for they sat up as he approached. Haril glanced at his shrunken features, almost hidden by the long matted hair which straggled down to his shoulders, and turned to Brond. 'So why have you brought me here?'

'Don't you recognise me, Haril?' the young man murmured.

Haril stared closely at the thin face with its sallow skin and gaunt, dark eyes, and suddenly something in him seemed to burst.

'It's been a long time,' the young man smiled. 'But you've not changed much, brother.'

'Torm!'

For a moment, Haril was unable to move. Then he ran forward and clasped his young brother to his breast. Tears of joy sprang to his eyes.

'I would have wakened you earlier,' Torm said. 'But we thought you should rest after the beating they gave you.'

Haril stood back and looked at him, still keeping his hands on his shoulders.

'I can hardly believe it.'

'I'm not surprised you didn't recognise me. But I knew you, as soon as I saw you fighting with that man.'

Haril didn't know whether to laugh or cry. Gentle Torm – he had always felt closer to him than any other member of the family. Haril had been the adventurous one, but it was Torm who always seemed to understand so much more, who would look into a person's eyes and know what they were thinking so that few people ever told him an untruth. It was Torm who nursed the animals when they were sick, and it was to him that people turned when they were in trouble although he never said very much. He was three years younger than Haril, and yet there was about him a wisdom and a simple goodness that was beyond mere age. Everyone in the village had loved him and felt the need to protect him because he was small and weaker than all the others. And yet, merely by being there, it was as if he protected them in return. No one felt afraid in Torm's presence, not of the dark or of the strange and nameless fears that sometimes came in the dead of night and caused men to shutter their doors and crouch round their fires for comfort.

Haril remembered a time when, as boys guarding their father's flock of sheep in the hills, a savage wolf had crept up behind them, its eyes red and half-mad from hunger. Haril, usually the brave one, had run away in terror, forgetting Torm, forgetting the sheep. When at last he turned, he had seen Torm walking slowly towards the animal staring at him, armed with no more than a little stick. He might have been talking to him for his lips were moving, but Haril was too far away to hear. And it was the wolf who backed away, snarling, and eventually turned and slunk off with its tail drooping. And when Haril returned, full of shame, Torm thanked him for going away to try and get help and never said a word about the incident to anyone.

Now, looking at Torm after so many years, seeing the signs of so much suffering, the calloused, twisted hands that had once been so gentle, the thin, starved body, Haril felt an anger that was even more terrible than before.

'How did you get to this place?' he asked harshly.

'The warriors came,' Torm replied. 'We offered them shelter – you remember, it was always our custom. Then they took all the men who were fit, and the others ... the others ...'

His voice trailed off and a look of horror came into his eyes.

'I know.' Haril said quickly. 'I saw when I came back to the village. Was it Karn?'

Torm shook his head. 'Vardon sent them. Karn was brought here later, after his own village had been raided.'

Haril clenched his fists. 'If only I had known. I could have killed Vardon with my own hands. And instead of that, I was helping him.'

'Your friend has told me about it,' Torm turned to Brond who was standing a few steps away. 'You're lucky to have such a friend, brother.'

Brond stepped forward. 'You must rest, both of you. There will be time for more talk tomorrow.'

Torm gave a short laugh and Haril was shocked to hear the bitterness and despair in it. 'Not during the day. There is time for nothing but work. Malik sees to that.'

'Tell me first about our father,' Haril asked eagerly. 'Is he also here?'

'He was. But he died – oh, I don't know when. Several moons ago. There are only a few from our village left.'

He spoke in an even, almost casual voice, betraying no feeling. As well as sorrow at hearing the words, Haril felt pained at Torm's apparent lack of concern.

'Is that all you have to say?' he said harshly.

'You are new here,' Torm said quietly. 'There is so much suffering that death is a blessed release. We are glad for those who die, especially if it is quick. There is no other way out.'

'There must be,' Haril cried.

'Some have tried. You saw what's left of them on your way down.'

'But we must do something.'

'The only way is to work as hard as you can and keep out of Malik's way. Unless you want to try to become one of the overseers.'

'I will not make that mistake again,' Haril declared indignantly.

Torm smiled wearily. 'People change when they come here,' he said softly. 'And now I must rest, brother. I'm so tired. We will talk further tomorrow night.'

He lay back on the hard rock and almost immediately his eyes closed and he was asleep. Haril went to touch him but Brond held him back. 'We must rest, also.'

'Torm was the best of us all,' Haril said harshly. 'And now look at him. It is not only his body that is broken. It is the spirit inside him as well.'

Brond looked down at the sleeping figure. 'You may be right. But from what I have heard, I do not think so.'

'What have you heard?'

'That he is known as a good man,' Brond said shortly. 'Come – leave him in peace.'

They returned to their sleeping places. As Haril lay down, he felt once again the pain that had been all but forgotten in the excitement of finding Torm alive. He gritted his teeth. Whatever Torm said, there must be some way of escape. Torm had been here too long; he had lost his will to do anything. But he, Haril, would find a way. He must. It was

with that thought in his mind that exhaustion
overtook him and he fell into a deep sleep.

*

It amused Malik, the chief overseer, to put Haril
and Brond to work on the same stone that was being
cut by Karn. As Malik led them to that section of
the cliff face on the first day after their arrival and
roughly pushed them forward, Karn cringed away
from Haril.

'Keep him away,' he whined. 'He tried to kill
me.'

Malik laughed loudly and flicked his whip
towards Karn, driving him back against the cliff.
'He won't try that again. Unless he wants another
flogging. Eh?' He turned sharply to Haril.

Haril shook his head. 'I made a mistake
yesterday.'

Malik looked disappointed; he had relished the
feud. 'Get on with your work. I'll be back to see
what such a great stone mason can do.'

He strode away, shouting to the men working
further along the cliff. Haril picked up one of the
flints and a larger rock with which to strike it, aware
that Karn was watching him uneasily. Haril had no
liking for the former hunter. He remembered the
way Karn and his men had treated the forest people,
although all that hatred seemed a lifetime ago. But
he felt a twinge of guilt for believing Karn had been
responsible for raiding his village. And turning

round and looking at him now, at the stooped back and haggard features of the man he had once known as a proud hunter, Haril could not help feeling pity for him as well as contempt.

'There's no quarrel between us,' he said.

Karn stared at him. His watery, blood-shot eyes betrayed fear but also a hint of cunning. 'I know you,' he muttered. 'You ran away from our village with the forest girl.'

'That was a long time ago. You've nothing to fear from me now.'

'Then why did you attack me?'

'I thought ... Well, that doesn't matter. I was wrong. It won't happen again.'

Haril turned his attention to the cliff face. Karn continued to look at him suspiciously for a while, then returned to his work, mumbling under his breath.

The stone they were cutting from the cliff was oblong in shape and parallel to the ground. The various types of rock were distinguished by lines which ran the length of the face, separating one layer from another. Such a line was level with Haril's knees, which marked one side of the required stone. The top side, which they were chipping away from the cliff, was level with his shoulders. When this had been cut to the depth required – rather like the wedge made when felling a tree, only large enough for men to crawl inside –

the next operation would be to cut down vertically. Then the ends would be cut away and the roughly hewn pillar was ready to be pulled away from the cliff. Haril guessed that the side at the bottom would not have to be cut but could be split by wooden wedges, following the natural layer of the rock.

Brond was already at work, chipping at the cliff with a sharp piece of flint. Haril joined him. Little splinters of stone flew back from the cliff and every so often landed with a stinging force in their eyes. It helped to keep the eyelids narrowed but even this did not give complete protection.

It was after one such occurrence, when Haril had stepped back from the cliff with a gasp, rubbing dust from his eyes and waiting for them to stop watering, that he noticed the crack. It was at the bottom of the stone, near the line that marked the natural strata. It was no wider than a strand of hair and it was not surprising none of the other slaves – semi-blinded from flying chips as they were – had noticed it. Neither they nor the guards would have understood its significance anyway. Haril bent down and examined it closely. There was no way of being certain. It might be merely a surface fracture. Or it might extend right through the stone, in which case at some point during the cutting operation, the stone would split in two.

'See this, Brond?' Haril pointed to the crack.

Brond looked down at it, creasing his eyes. 'I can't see anything.'

Haril turned to Karn. 'Who marks out where to cut the stones?'

'Korth does it himself,' Karn muttered.

'Then I think he has made a mistake with this one.'

Karn glanced around fearfully. 'The priests never make a mistake,' he whispered. 'You don't know what you're saying. If anyone should hear ...'

'If anyone should hear what?' a voice said loudly. Malik was standing behind them, hands on his hips.

Haril pointed again to the crack. 'There's a flaw in the stone. It could split at any time. Now, if we moved along here and made another cut ...'

Malik wasn't even listening. 'You want to tell Korth how to do his work?' he sneered, uncoiling his whip threateningly. 'Get back to work unless you want some more of this.'

Haril went back to his cutting. Malik stood watching him for a moment before striding away. When he was gone, Haril turned to Brond. 'I just hope I'm wrong.'

'Why? What if the stone does break? It will be one less for Vardon.'

'It's still a pity to waste such beautiful stone.'

Brond shook his head. 'Won't you ever learn?' he said gruffly. 'Nothing that is evil can have real beauty.'

Chapter Eleven

As the days passed with little to distinguish one from the other, time became a monotonous routine of work and sleep. Even the periodic beatings which none could escape, however hard they worked, became dulled as the body lost its capacity to feel. The slaves existed in a state of lethargy, dreamlike and unthinking. They would rise with the sun, eat a bowl of thin soup prepared from the meagre supplies of vegetables and tough meat sent down by the guards, toil all day whatever the weather with only a few brief rest periods, and eat another bowl of soup at night before huddling in caves to sleep. They seldom spoke and there were few friendships, even between those who had known each other in the world outside. In fact, it barely seemed that such a world could exist. Memories faded, in much the same way that bodies became wasted and diseased and eventually sank down into pathetic little bundles of death, to be dragged away by the overseers and thrown into a large pit some distance from the guards' camp.

Even the presence of women amongst them caused few quarrels. When a man had used one of them for a fleeting moment of lust, he didn't care if other men might take her afterwards. There were no possessions to fight over, or to give as a token of endearment. The women were the slaves of slaves. Babies were born and as soon as they could walk they were put to work. They lived for less time even than those who had been captured and brought to the quarry from outside.

Haril saw little of his brother after the first night. He was working in another part of the quarry, and at night sleep was the only merciful relief from exhaustion and pain. But he heard about Torm. About the way he had tried to ease the suffering of his comrades and comfort them in death or, once, had given his own food ration to a sick child.

To begin with, thought of escape was never far from Haril's mind. He studied every detail of the hell they were in. The cliffs which made up three sides of the quarry were smooth and sheer, reaching up to the height of fifty men. There was no escape that way without ropes lowered from the top – and even if they had ropes, there was no way of getting out to use them. The only way out was up the slope and that was always guarded at the top by soldiers; they were armed and the slaves were not. Even if they could, by sheer force of numbers, kill the overseers, who slept in wooden huts at the bottom of the slope, and take their clubs and whips, they could not match swords and spears. And the penalty for attacking an overseer was too terrible to contemplate.

One man, driven beyond reason by hunger and torment, had knocked an overseer to the ground, taken hold of his club and run up the slope shouting wildly. The other slaves had watched him in silence. No one tried to stop him. When he reached the top, brandishing the club and still shouting, one of the guards had walked forward and thrust his sword into the man's forearm. The man had screamed and dropped the club. He had been roughly seized by the other guards. A pointed wooden stake had been set into the ground where all could see and the man impaled on it in an upright position. But not so deep that he would die quickly. It had taken most of the day before his screams gradually faded and his legs stopped their grotesque kicking. The following day, a similar fate had befallen the overseer who had been foolish enough to allow himself to be attacked. There was never any shortage of recruits for new overseers among the slaves. It was not surprising that they were even more cruel than the guards.

As Haril realised how hopeless it was, determination gave way to desperation, and desperation to despair. Finally, even despair began to merge into an almost tranquil thoughtless state. It was so much easier not to think, to accept that in the last resort there was one escape at least, through death.

Much of the time when he was not working Brond spent examining the caves. Some of them were very

179

large and extended deep into the cliffs, but it had not taken Haril long to discover that all of them were blocked off at some point. There were no tunnels leading out of the quarry, a fact which the guards had obviously checked long ago.

'Why do you waste so much time in the caves?' Haril demanded angrily.

'There are some interesting kinds of rock here,' Brond replied evasively.

'You stupid old man. I know more about rock than you do, and what use is that? It doesn't help get us out of here.'

Brond shrugged his shoulders and moved away. Haril felt immediately ashamed of his outburst. The lack of food and the hard work had taken an even greater toll on Brond; his hair was now thin and pure white, his body stooped forward, and he coughed continually so that the others had made him sleep in one of the caves by himself so he would not keep them awake. It was the cave in which the dead bodies were kept before being removed from the quarry.

Work on the stone that Haril was helping to cut progressed slowly. From his knowledge of the temple and what had been done there so far, he knew it would be one of the final stones to be put in place, if not the last, possibly surmounting the archway at the entrance. It was hard and smooth to the touch, with a blue-black radiance that seemed to come from the very heart of the mountain, and Haril often found himself almost glad to be working on it. Chipping away the surrounding rock, a few fragments at a time, he also knew it would take more than a year to complete, and a similar time to drag it to the temple.

Once, when he was intent on one of the corners, taking care to retain the right shape, he became aware of a stir behind him. He looked round and saw Korth watching him, the same bitter half smile on his lips. Selem was with him, together with a group of guards and Haril was surprised to see how much he had aged, not realising how much more so that could be said of him. There was a strange expression in the young priest's eyes as he looked round at the filth and degradation of the quarry. And when his eyes met Haril's, there was pity in them as well as anger.

'I have heard you work well,' Korth wheezed in his high-pitched voice.

'We would all work better with more food,' Haril retorted.

Korth laughed. 'Food is harder to find than slaves. But I am pleased with you, Haril. Perhaps we will soon make you an overseer.'

It had been in Haril's mind to tell Korth about the hairline fracture in the stone. But the priest's words dissuaded him. He remembered with shame how he had served Vardon.

'I wish you to see a stone which we are about to send to the temple,' Korth continued. 'Come with me.'

Haril put down his tools and followed the group across the quarry.

'Back to work the rest of you,' Malik shouted to the others, anxious to show his authority. As Haril passed by, Malik grinned at him. The overseer obviously felt that Haril might have some influence from now on. Haril looked away, sickened.

In the centre of the quarry was the stone that had been cut. It was a perfect specimen. The guards had brought down ropes made of tree fibres and the slaves were now tying them round the stone in preparation for dragging it out of the quarry. But just as Korth was asking Haril's opinion of the stone and whether it was exactly what Vardon required, shouting broke out behind them. They turned. Malik was in the middle of a group of slaves, screaming at the top of his voice and furiously whipping at someone on the ground.

The guards ran forward, swords drawn, and drove their way through to Malik. Haril followed.

The man stretched out in the dirt was Brond.

'What has happened?' Korth demanded.

Malik pointed to the cliff face. The stone had splintered along the crack. It was now only three-quarters of its original size.

'This clumsy fool has broken the stone,' Malik cried out, his voice shaking from anger and fear. 'He struck it in the wrong place.'

Haril stepped forward. 'That is not true,' he said. 'There was a crack in the rock. I told Malik about it long ago.'

Malik's face became purple with rage. 'He lies. He is trying to protect his friend.'

Korth raised his hand for silence. His voice was ominously calm. 'I marked out that stone myself,' he said.

'Anyone could have missed seeing it,' Haril said carefully, aware that Brond was now trying to stagger to his feet. 'If Malik had done something about it when I told him, we could have cut from another part of the rock.'

'He did not tell me,' Malik shouted desperately. 'Do you think I would not have told you, master, if what he says is true?'

Korth stared at the trembling overseer for a moment, then turned to Haril. 'You are trying to save your friend,' he accused.

'No.'

'Then why did you not tell me about the crack while we were talking just now?'

Haril hesitated, unable to think what to say. And then it was too late. Korth signalled to the guards, and they gathered round Brond, raining blows on him and kicking him to the ground again. Haril tried to run forward, but he was held by two of the overseers.

'I can save the stone,' he cried.

'How?' Korth demanded.

'We can cut further back into the rock to make it the right size.'

Korth frowned thoughtfully. 'It might work.'

'Tell your men to stop. Or I will not work again, though you kill me.'

Korth smiled. 'You are a fool, but you have courage. Very well. Enough.'

He called out to the guards. They stepped back from the bleeding, broken wreck on the ground. Haril ran forward and knelt beside Brond. His face was battered and almost unrecognisable but he was still breathing faintly.

'If the work takes any longer than usual,' Korth called out as he turned to leave, 'you will suffer for it.'

Haril reached beneath Brond to lift him up. The old man was surprisingly light. His bones felt thin and brittle. They were broken in several places.

Haril carried him towards the cave where he slept. Because of its association with the dead, no one other than Brond ever went inside. Whispers of strange spirits were told about it. Haril looked round at the slaves. Now that Korth and the guards had left the quarry, they were drifting back to work.

'Will someone help me?' Haril cried out.

No one answered. Then Torm stepped forward. Without saying anything he put his arms under Brond and helped Haril carry him into the cave. At that moment, Malik came up to them.

'Put him down and get back to work,' he shouted, lifting his whip.

Haril looked the overseer straight in the eye, trying to control the rage that was building up inside him. 'We are going to look after this man, and then we will work, Malik,' he said evenly. 'And if you try to stop us, I swear I will kill you.'

Malik hesitated, seeing the determination on Haril's face. 'Be quick, then,' he growled. 'If you don't save that stone ...'

The cave stank of putrefaction. As gently as they could, they put Brond down on a heap of straw at the back. Torm fetched some rags and water and bathed the blood from his wounds. Haril carefully stretched out the old man's limbs, straightening the bones that had been broken. Brond's breath was coming in short gasps.

'I don't think he'll live for long,' Torm murmured.

'He's stronger than you think,' Haril replied, binding a rag round the gash in one of Brond's legs. He didn't want even to think of the possibility of Brond dying.

'Torm is right.' The words came in a barely audible whisper. Brond had regained consciousness. His face was deathly pale.

'Lie still, old man,' Haril said softly. 'You have recovered from worse than this.'

'Not this time, Haril.'

There was pain in the words, and certainty. Haril felt a thickness gathering at the back of his throat. 'I won't let you die,' he said fiercely. 'Not in this place.'

Brond's eyes closed again. 'Just a few days,' he muttered, slowly sinking back into unconsciousness. 'That's all I want ... a few days ...'

Torm looked up at Haril. 'What does he mean?'

'His mind is wondering.' Haril blinked back the tears that had come to his eyes. 'We must save him.'

'In this place, it is not such a bad thing to die.'

For the rest of that day and well into the night they nursed Brond. It was early the following morning, when the first light of dawn was beginning to reach the gloomy, dank depths of the quarry, that Brond re-awoke. Haril and Torm had fallen asleep by his side. With a great effort he reached out and touched them.

'Wake up,' he whispered urgently.

They were instantly alert. 'How do you feel?' Haril asked.

'That does not matter. We have much to do and there is little time.'

There was an unreal sense of purpose about him. Torm glanced at Haril and shook his head slightly.

'First, give me water,' Brond continued.

Haril lifted his shoulders and put a bowl to his lips. He drank eagerly; some of the water trickled down his chin and on to his emaciated chest. Then he lay back, breathing heavily.

'At the back of the cave ... a large pot,' he muttered. 'Bring it to me.'

'You mustn't talk,' Haril said gently. 'Try to rest.'

'Do what I say.'

Torm stood up. 'I'll go,' he whispered.

Haril examined the old man's wounds. They had stopped bleeding but in a dozen places the flesh was open and raw. A young man might recover from such wounds, his bones might mend again in some misshapen manner. But in his heart Haril knew that what Torm said was true; in such a weakened state, Brond did not have long to live.

Torm returned, carrying a large earthenware pot, the kind used by the women for cooking. It was filled with the crushed fragments of a reddish-brown rock.

'I have seen rock like that before,' Haril said, taking a handful. Some of the pieces splintered like slate when he clenched his fist and ran them through his fingers.

Brond nodded. 'There is a layer of it in some of the caves. In here, as well.'

'It's useless. It breaks when you strike it with flint. Look, I can crush it between my fingers.'

'That is what I have been doing,' Brond said. 'That's why I came into this cave, where none could see me.'

Haril said: 'They are all afraid to come into the cave of the dead.' He remembered the stories he had heard of the ghosts of those who had once lived. In this unholy place it was only too easy to believe there might be some truth in them.

'You waste time,' Brond said impatiently. 'You must do as I say. Dig a trench in the ground – as long and as thick as your arm.'

Now Haril was certain that Brond had lost his reason. He looked at Torm. Brond saw the movement.

'I am not mad,' he said angrily. 'You want a chance to escape from this place, don't you?'

'Yes, but ...'

'You, Torm ... go and gather as much wood as you can and bring it here.'

Every day, some of the women were allowed out of the quarry, under guard, to collect wood for the fires. There was a large pile of it outside. Torm hesitated, but there was something in Brond's voice that commanded obedience. He left the cave.

While he was away, Haril dug the trench, scooping the earth out with a lump of flint. Then, according to Brond's instructions, he poured in the fragments of rock until they were level with the ground.

'Now build a fire over it,' Brond ordered. His voice was shaky.

Haril built the fire with twigs that were in the cave, lighting it by striking a flint. Torm returned with an armful of wood which he placed close to Brond so that the old man could feed the fire without having to move much.

The fire began to crackle and spit. Brond reached painfully into a crevice in the rock beside him and took out a strange-looking object, made from two flat pieces of wood and the skin of an animal shaped roughly into a round bag. Haril stared at it curiously.

'What is it?' he asked.

Brond did not reply. He took the two ends of wood in his hands and began pushing them together and then apart again. Haril felt a cold breeze coming from a hole in the bag as it was continuously inflated and then deflated. He glanced at Torm who was also watching closely, a puzzled frown creasing his forehead.

Turning slowly on his side, Brond pointed the hole at the fire.

'It will blow out the flames,' Torm exclaimed.

Brond shook his head as he began pumping the bag again.

'No. See?'

As the air blew against the twigs, they flared up and became redder with heat.

'It makes the fire hotter,' Brond murmured.

Torm nodded. 'It is a wonderful device.'

'An old bronzesmith's trick, that is all. And now, you must go back to work, both of you.'

'No, we will stay here with you,' Haril cried.

Brond shook his head. 'They will become suspicious. Come back this evening.'

'What is it you are trying to do?' Torm asked.

'We must wait and see, first. If it does not work ... well, it is worth trying.'

Slowly and painfully, Brond put some more wood on the fire. Outside, there were sounds of the slaves stirring to life again. They could hear Malik shouting for work to commence. Torm put his hand on Haril's shoulder. 'Come brother ...'

Brond smiled as he lay back, his eyes half-closed. 'You have a wisdom and goodness beyond your years, Torm,' he murmured. 'Your brother does not have such wisdom, but he has courage and the spirit to seek beyond the commonplace. You must always be true to each other. Together, there is much you could achieve.'

He spoke with the prophesy of a dying man. Haril felt a deep anguish inside him as he stumbled out of the cave, followed by Torm.

All day they worked hard at the damaged stone, giving Malik no cause for complaint. Several times he came and stood over them, glowering his hatred and waiting for his chance to find a mistake that would give him reason to drag them before Korth. But they made no such mistake and at the end of the day he could only grunt and nod for them to line up with the others to collect their meagre allowance of food.

They brought a bowl of the foul-smelling soup to Brond. The old man was lying where they had left him, his eyes still closed, and it seemed that he had not moved. But the fire was still burning brightly and there was little left of the pile of wood by his side.

Torm lifted his shoulders while Haril fed what he could into his mouth. Brond was weaker than ever, the pallor of death on his face. When he had drunk what he could, he looked at the fire.

'Now it is time,' he whispered. 'Take away the fire.'

'But you'll be cold.' Haril protested.

'You still argue with me?'

Haril raised his eyes despairingly, then picked up a stick and knocked away the pieces of burning wood. Once separated from the internal heat of the ashes, the flames quickly died out. The embers that remained glowed an orange-red. Haril brushed them away with the stick. Underneath, the trench was filled with something that was also red but gradually became black as it cooled.

'Pour water on it,' Brond said slowly. His voice was now dry and faint so that they had to bend close to hear him.

The water hissed and steamed as it came into contact with what was in the trench. Haril began to dig the earth away. There in the trench where he had put the fragments of rock was something which looked like a long, black, smooth piece of wood.

'Lift it out,' Brond said.

Haril reached under and lifted it up. It was still warm, but hard and surprisingly heavy.

'I do not understand,' he muttered.

'Strike that piece of rock over there.'

Haril held the object at one end and hit a chunk of rock lying on the floor. He expected the thing to shatter into pieces. But instead, there was a dull clang and it was the rock that broke.

Brond sighed. 'It is done.'

Haril stared at what he held in his hand. His arm ached from the jarring blow.

'What is it?'

'It is a secret that one day will conquer the earth,' Brond murmured. 'It is called iron.'

Torm took it from Haril and began to swing it to and fro. Excitement showed in his eyes. He felt the smooth surface with his fingers. 'It is not rock at all,' he said. 'It is like bronze. A new metal.'

Brond nodded. 'I first heard about it in another country. A long time ago and far from here. When it is still hot and soft, it can be hammered into any shape you want. It will always stay in that shape when it becomes cold and hard.'

'Why didn't you make it before?' Haril cried, catching Torm's excitement. 'You are a worker in metal. It is like magic.'

'It is ugly,' Brond replied. 'It is not soft and beautiful like bronze. But it is harder and much stronger. Men will use it, but for evil I fear and not for good.'

'But think of what you could do with it. You could ...' Haril broke off, his eyes gleaming.

'Yes. Tell me ... how do you use a bronze sword?'

'You thrust forward with it,' Torm said quickly. 'Like a spear. If you strike sideways, the sword will bend.'

'Iron will not bend. It will not break, even against the hardest flint. It is stronger than anything else in the world.'

'We can arm ourselves and fight the guards and get away from this place.'

'That is why I have given you this knowledge.'

'Their bronze will be like a child's toy against this.'

Brond struggled into a sitting position. 'I have put the secret of the future into your hands,' he said urgently. 'But you must promise me ... use it only for good.'

'You can make sure of that when we take you out of here,' Haril said, crouching down to support Brond's shoulders. 'You have made it possible.'

'Promise me,' Brond repeated.

Torm knelt down by his other side. 'We promise,' he said.

'And you will not show the secret to anyone else?'

'Never.'

'It will happen all the same,' Brond sighed. 'Other men will come with iron weapons and there will be wars more terrible than the world has ever seen.'

'Now you must rest,' Haril said gently. 'We have much to do. And you must be strong for when we escape.'

Brond shook his head slowly. 'My time has come. You must not sorrow for me. All my life I have worked at what I love and made things of beauty.'

His voice trailed away and a tiny trickle of blood fell down his chin. Haril cradled the old man in his arms and there was a tightness in his chest as if it would burst.

'Brond, Brond,' he sobbed, tears running unashamedly down his cheeks.

The old eyes flickered open and the ghost of a smile crossed Brond's face. 'It is good to have a son at the end,' he whispered. 'You are headstrong and you will always go your own way. But just remember some of the things that old Brond has told you.'

They buried him there, in the cave of the dead. And even in death, Brond did one last service for them. They did not tell anyone he was dead and it gave them an excuse to come into the cave at night and begin forging weapons with the knowledge Brond had given them. And in his heartbreak and loneliness, Haril felt some sense of comfort from the little mound of earth in the corner and the feeling that some part of the old man's spirit was still there to guide them.

Chapter Twelve

Now that they understood the process of melting the iron ore, Haril and Torm were able to work out improvements. They dug the earthen moulds more closely to the shape of a sword, and they found they could put a sharper edge to the blade by reheating it and hammering it with lumps of iron which they made for that purpose. A fire did not produce sufficient heat unless it burned for at least a day and even then they had to make it hotter by using the crude bellows. It was slow, arduous work, especially after a daytime of labour, and the strain soon began to tell in the dark circles under their eyes and the hollowness of their cheeks. But now they had something to hope for. The hammering might have disturbed the guards, but Haril found an answer to that problem. He suggested that they should take it in turns to work on the damaged stone at night. Malik readily agreed. Fires were kept going for the slaves to see by and this meant bringing in more wood which also helped by giving Haril and Torm a bigger supply of fuel. The other slaves were too afraid of the guards to make any protest against Haril.

He and Torm discussed the possibility of recruiting others to help them but they decided against it. The slaves had become so abject over the years that it was doubtful if any of them had the will to do anything. There was also the danger that someone would inform on them.

In the camp at the top of the slope there were, as far as they could gather, about sixty guards, in addition to Korth and Selem. There were as many overseers in the quarry and about four hundred male slaves. Haril had thought at one time that if all the slaves armed themselves with rocks and attacked together in one large force, at least some of them would be able to get away. But the biggest problem was the chains attached between their ankles which made it impossible to run or move faster than a kind of shuffle. Fewer than a hundred of the slaves had ever known freedom. Some, like Haril and Torm and Karn, had been taken prisoner outside and brought to the quarry to work; all the others had been born in captivity and knew no other life. It was rumoured that, long ago, an attempt to escape had been made. They had all perished miserably. Now, they accepted the state they were in; even the idea of resistance was unthinkable.

The slaves needed something in the way of weapons, that they could see and hold in their hands, rather than the vague idea of a rushed attack . That something would be swords made of iron. And these swords, as Haril discovered after careful experiments, could easily break through the bronze chains that bound their ankles.

The time came when Haril and Torm had made sixteen swords. They had decided that at least thirty would be required. Even that number would still leave them with odds of two to one against the guards, but the superiority of their weapons should give them the advantage.

Then, late one night, just as they were pouring the rock fragments into an earthen mould, a shadow fell across the mouth of the cave. Etched against the light from the fires outside was the figure of one of the overseers. He was a small, thin man, not so obviously brutal as Malik but even more hated in some ways for his petty cruelties and his sadistic delight in subjecting the women to every possible degradation. It was the twisted body of a woman that he now carried and threw into the cave, ready to be dragged away the next day. Unfortunately, just as he was about to leave, one of the fires flared up and its brightness shone into the back of the cave. The overseer saw Haril and Torm bending over their work.

'Where is the old man?' he demanded.

The brothers looked up quickly, their hearts beating fast.

'He ... went outside,' Torm replied, thinking fast. 'He needed to exercise his legs.'

'If he can walk, he can work,' the overseers said. 'I can use another man. Which way did he go?'

Haril and Torm looked at one another. It wouldn't take the overseers long to discover that Brond was not in the quarry.

'Speak up, you dogs,' the man shouted, stepping further into the cave, his annoyance overcoming his repugnance at entering the feared place. Then he saw the bowl and the pile of rock chippings and the lump of iron that Haril and Torm used as an anvil. 'What are you doing there?'

'Come and see for yourself,' Haril said, quietly picking up one of the swords and hiding it behind his back.

The overseer lifted his wooden club threateningly and walked towards them. He caught sight of the swords lying to one side and his eyes opened wide in astonishment. 'Where did you get ...' he began. He turned to run from the cave, shouting.

Haril shuffled forward as quickly as the chains would allow, holding the sword high. The man turned with surprising agility and as Haril struck, he held out the club so that it took the weight of the blow. The shock jarred Haril's arm so much that he nearly dropped the sword. Seeing his chance, the overseer rushed at Haril, swinging the club ferociously. Haril only just managed to dodge out of the way. He swept the sword down again and this time it caught the man between his neck and shoulder. The blade sank into yielding flesh, opening a great rent down to his chest. A look of puzzlement came over his face, then he crashed to the ground. He was dead.

Haril and Torm looked down at the body and at the blood pouring from the wound. They had known the strength of the iron, but this first example of its force as a weapon left them shattered. No sword of bronze could have delivered such a crushing blow.

'It will not be long before he is missed,' Torm said after a while.

'We could bury him.'

Torm shook his head. 'They would search. We cannot hide all this.'

'That leaves only one answer,' Haril said slowly.

'Yes. The time is now.'

They looked steadily at one another, then smiled and gripped each other's arms.

'Either we escape, or we die in the attempt,' Haril said.

'Good luck to you brother.'

'And to you.'

'You look after the weapons,' Torm said. 'I'll go and fetch Karn, as we planned.'

*

It was only with the greatest reluctance that Karn was persuaded to come to the cave. He stood at the entrance and peered inside suspiciously.

'What is it you want with me?' he demanded.

'We have something to show you.' Haril called out.

'You come out here,' Karn retorted.

Haril picked up one of the swords and walked towards Karn. The former hunter stared at it incredulously and backed away.

'Do you want everyone to see?' Haril said. 'Come inside. Here, take it yourself if you are afraid.'

He threw it at Karn's feet. It fell with a dull clang. Slowly, almost afraid to touch it, Karn bent down and picked it up; he felt the edge of the blade, and took his hand away quickly when a small cut appeared. Torm led him unprotestingly into the cave.

Karn looked around and stared wonderingly at the pile of swords. There was nothing else. Haril had destroyed the mould and all evidence of how the swords had been made.

'What is it?' Karn asked after a long pause.

'A new kind of metal,' Torm replied. 'Stronger than bronze. Try it for yourself.'

Karn swung the sword experimentally, then struck gently at one of the rocks. When the blade did not bend or break, he hit it again, harder. A large chip of rock broke off.

'Where did you get it?' Karn whispered.

'That is no matter,' Haril said. 'Will you fight with us to escape from this place?'

Karn frowned, hardly able to comprehend such an idea.

'Escape?'

'Of course,' Haril said impatiently. 'Or do you wish to die here as a slave, like the others.'

'No one has ever escaped from here,' Karn muttered.

'They have not had weapons such as these.'

Karn looked at the sword again. 'It is truly a thing of wonder.' As he became more accustomed to it and held it with more confidence, a cunning look came into his eyes. 'How did you make them?' he asked again.

'It is a secret that none but us will ever know,' Torm said quietly. 'Sixteen men armed with these, and the other slaves with rocks and sticks should be enough to overcome the guards.'

Karn nodded thoughtfully. 'But where to find sixteen men with any courage left ...'

'There are five from our village, who may fight,' Haril said. 'And the three of us. That leaves eight. Are there any among your people who would hunt again as free men, or are they no better than dogs who would curl up and die in this hole?'

'We have not been men for a long time,' Karn muttered. 'They would need a sign to show the power of these weapons.'

'That is what Haril and I thought. Will you help us?'

Karn thought deeply. 'I believed I could never leave here,' he said slowly. 'But now the thought of it stirs my blood. Yes, I will help. When?'

'Tomorrow. When the sun has risen over the hills. Its light will be in the eyes of the guards when we climb the slope.'

There was a long silence as each of them tried to imagine an event of such enormity.

'Leave the sword here, and tell no one,' Haril told Karn. 'Then come with your men when you see our signal.'

Karn put the sword reluctantly with the others and turned to leave the cave. 'Until tomorrow then,' he said.

'And remember,' Torm added, 'it is the only chance any of us will ever have. If we fail, we will die. But at least it will not be as slaves.'

Karn nodded, and left the cave.

'Can we trust him?' Haril said.

Torm shrugged. 'We can't trust any of them. The years in this place have sapped their will. We can only hope.'

They lay down to rest. The simple plan they had agreed upon had been discussed until there was nothing left to say. It was no longer time for words.

*

Early the following morning they joined the rest of the slaves working on the cliff face. The stone had progressed sufficiently to enable each of them in turn to clamber into the wedge-shaped ledge cut in the cliff and cut along the back. It was gruelling work, cramped into such a position until muscles and sinews screamed with pain. It was ironic to know that the whole operation could be done ten times faster and certainly more easily by use of axes made of iron. Haril wondered how long it would be before such implements were in general use. They would transform the world, as Brond had said.

Slowly, the sun rose over the hills above them and the shadows retreated down the slope. It was now time. Haril looked behind him. All around the cliffs the slaves were hard at work. Women were bringing in fresh supplies of wood for the fires. The overseers with their whips were shouting as usual. It was a scene Haril knew would always be etched in his memory. Malik stood alone at the bottom of the slope, hands on hips in his usual arrogant stance, his eyes darting to the left and right to see everything that was going on.

Haril slowly drew the sword that he had hidden under his ragged clothes. He grasped the hilt firmly in his right hand and made his way towards Malik.

'What do you want?' Malik shouted. 'Get back to work.'

'Not this time, Malik,' Haril retorted. He lifted the sword and struck the chain between his ankles. It broke easily. His heart was pounding furiously.

There was no going back now. Malik's mouth gaped open. 'How did you do that?' he whispered.

Haril steadily walked towards him. 'You have killed many men, Malik. How many? Twenty? Fifty? More? It's a pity you can only die once.'

The overseer's face reddened and twisted into ugly lines. He held up his club in one hand and with the other drew back his whip. 'You will plead for death before I am finished with you,' he snarled.

Some of the nearby slaves stared at the two men, vacantly and without comprehension. Malik jumped forward and the whip lashed out and coiled around Haril's body. Haril had been prepared for it but even so he could not help staggering from the force of the blow. Then he swept the sword down and cut the whip. Malik was left with only one handle in his hand. He stared at the sword incredulously. But he was not a coward and with a fierce cry aimed a mighty blow at Haril with his club. Haril sprang to one side and struck out with the sword. It cut into Malik's arm. Malik fell back, the blood running down to his fingers.

Haril turned as three of the overseers who were nearest ran towards him. He slashed out with the sword. One of them fell to the ground with his throat severed. Another managed to land a stinging cut across Haril's shoulders before Haril despatched him with a quick thrust to the body. The third backed away and shouted for the others to come and help.

Now everyone in the quarry was staring, utter amazement on their faces. The slaves remained motionless but all the overseers who were present, about thirty of them, were advancing on Haril. Torm ran forward, his sword in hand, to stand back to back with Haril.

'Where is Karn?' Haril panted.

Torm pointed towards the cave. Karn was standing close by it with a small group of men, but as yet they were not making any move.

Perhaps the overseers thought that Haril and Torm were armed only with sticks. Perhaps they were so astonished at the idea that anyone should dare confront them that they did not realise the danger. In any event, they rushed forward to seize the two men, confident that their numbers would over power them. There was a confusion of shouting and swirling dust and the blades of two swords rising and falling in the air. When it cleared and about half of the men staggered back, the ground was littered with bodies and severed limbs.

'See ... we have weapons,' Haril shouted to the slaves. 'Karn will give you swords to break your chains. Pick up stones, anything you can find. Together we will fight our way from here. Death to the oppressors!'

There was a murmur from among the slaves, but no one moved. Torm looked towards the men of his village who had been captured with him.

'Join us,' he cried out. 'We have swords that can win against bronze. This is our day of freedom.'

The men shuffled their feet and looked at one another, but still no one ran forward. Malik had by now gathered all the overseers together. Slowly they advanced on the two men, but now they were armed with clubs and moved warily. Haril knew that if they made another rush, he and Torm would be overpowered. They might kill a few more of them, but two swords alone were no match against so many clubs and whips.

'Kill them,' Malik shouted frenziedly. 'There are only two of them. Kill them.'

Haril and Torm were now backed against the cliff, encircled by the overseers. At Malik's command, the overseers rushed forward. And it was at that moment, with a great shout, that Karn charged through the circle, flailing from side to side with his sword.

'Arm yourselves,' he cried, cutting a path through the overseers and joining Haril and Torm. 'We are slaves no longer.'

Fleetingly, Haril saw that the swords were piled up outside the cave. Some of the slaves were beginning to pick them up, holding them in awe, then breaking their chains and running to join the fight. Others picked up stones and began throwing them at the overseers, silently at first, then shouting triumphantly.

It was over very quickly. One by one the overseers fell, killed by sword cuts or knocked down and crushed with stones. The slaves took savage revenge against the men who had oppressed them for so long. Malik was beaten to death by fists and stones. At last, there were no more overseers left alive.

The men who were armed with swords gathered around Haril, Torm and Karn, the three leaders. Suddenly, the shouting died down. Haril saw the slaves were looking up at the slope. He turned also, remembering that the main battle was to come.

The guards were massed at the top of the slope, entirely blocking the way out. They all wore helmets and breastplates of bronze and carried bronze swords. The sun was shining full on them, reflecting back in a blaze of golden light. To one side, on top of the cliff, stood Korth and Selem.

'They are armed only with bronze,' Haril cried out. 'Bronze that is soft and bends like a willow. They cannot win against our swords of iron.'

'But there are many of them and few of us,' one of the men muttered.

'Fools,' Karn shouted. 'We are dead anyway, if we surrender now. Follow me. And the rest of you.

Pick up any weapons you can find and come with us.'

Led by Karn, who had shaken off his earlier timidity and was now something of the strong hunter that Haril remembered, the sixteen armed men made their way up the slope towards the assembled guards. The weapons in their hands and the knowledge of their miraculous power gave them courage. But when Haril glanced back, he saw that only a dozen or so of the other slaves were following them, carrying clubs they had taken from the overseers. The rest stood in fearful, huddled groups, like sheep awaiting slaughter.

The guards had the advantage of height, but the sun was in their eyes. Also, there was only room for about twenty of them to stand side by side, facing the slaves. The first onslaught, accompanied by fiendish yells, drove them back until the slaves reached the flat ground beyond. It was now that Haril fully realised how superior the iron swords were to bronze. They could slash up and down and from side to side whereas the guards could only thrust forward and even then their swords would often bend and had to be straightened by pressing them to the ground with the heel of a boot. The helmets and breastplates gave little protection against the weight of iron. But the guards had the advantage of numbers and, as the battle raged on, the slaves found themselves being encircled. Some of them were now facing the blinding sun.

From the cliff top, Korth was shouting feverishly to his men, urging them to greater efforts. Suddenly, another voice rang out. It was Selem.

'Enough,' he cried. 'There has been too much blood spilled in this place. Let the slaves through.'

A silence came over the camp. Slaves and guards alike stopped fighting and turned to Selem in wonderment. The young priest's eyes flashed.

'I do not know how it is the slaves are fighting, or with what strange weapons,' he cried out. 'But for a long time I have known this to be a place of evil. And so is the temple that Vardon enslaves men to build. Suffering such as I have seen here is not for the honour of the Sun-god. It is for the power of darkness which Vardon seeks to bring to the world.'

'Selem is right.' Another voice called out and Haril saw it was Gort, the giant who had brought him to the quarry. 'We are warriors, not murderers of women and old men. Let the slaves leave.'

No one moved. Then Korth screamed out in fury. He drew a knife from his robe and leapt upon Selem. It struck Selem in the shoulder. The young priest reached out and grasped Korth around the throat. They struggled backwards and forwards for several moments while everyone watched breathlessly. They were too far away for anyone to reach them in time, no matter which one they wanted to help. It was as if the decision was being fought out in front of their eyes.

Korth was strong and agile for his age. Slowly, he pressed Selem to the edge of the cliff. But with a great effort, Selem swung round and pushed. The old man staggered back, his arms grasping empty air. He gave a shrill cry as he tottered backwards towards the edge, unable to keep his balance. For a moment he was poised in space, grotesquely swinging his arms; then he fell, landing with a thud on the slope below the cliff. He slithered down a short way on the stones, then came to rest in a heap of rags and broken bones.

A tremendous shout went up. The guards backed away from the slaves and gathered around Gort. The slaves waved their swords in the air triumphantly.

'Well, Haril,' Gort called out. 'You are free to go or to fight. Which is it to be?'

Haril was standing with Torm and Karn. All of them bore wounds from the battle but none were serious.

'Selem is right. This place has seen enough blood.'

Gort nodded and turned to the guards. 'We will go to another part of the country. There is no place for us with Vardon.'

'Why not come with us?'

'And where do you go?'

'To the Temple of Stone.' It was Selem who answered, striding towards them from the cliff. His eyes were burning with some inner fire. 'There is an evil there which must be destroyed.'

'We want no more fighting,' Karn shouted. 'We want to return to our villages and our hunting.'

Some of the others shouted their agreement.

'Yes, and you will be hunted again and made slaves once more,' Selem cried. 'No one will be safe until Vardon is destroyed.'

'Have you forgotten what you have suffered?' Haril demanded angrily. 'Your villages burned to the ground, your women and children killed. Does their blood cry out for vengeance?'

Louder shouts of approval greeted his words. He walked a few steps away. Then he turned and faced the crowd. Its numbers were swollen now by the slaves who had crept fearfully up from the quarry.

'Those who would kill the tyrant, come with me,' he called out. 'It will not be easy, but we have weapons such as no one has ever seen before. Let the others depart in peace.'

Torm and Selem immediately came over and stood by his side. The others hesitated, then some of those also came over. Gort strode up to Haril. 'I would dearly like to fight with swords such as these,' he said.

'So you shall. And we will have more of them so that everyone is armed.'

'There will be much plunder in Vardon's camp,' Karn said, joining them.

'Yes,' Selem cried. 'The druid priests have riches beyond your dreams.'

'You are a priest, too,' Karn said spitefully.

'Not any longer. I renounce them with all my heart.'

Haril turned to him, frowning. 'We are not thieves,' he growled. 'We don't want men who merely seek plunder.'

'We want everyone we can get, Haril,' Selem said. 'Nothing matters but the destruction of the temple. We are threatened by powers even greater than you can imagine.'

At last, the guards and their former slaves had divided into two groups. The smaller one surrounded Haril; it included some of the guards, like Gort, who lived by fighting and were looking enviously at the iron swords. There were some of the younger slaves who burned for revenge. And there were others tempted by the plunder they might find.

The larger group split up into small parties, who gradually began to make their way across the plateau and down the mountain. Haril was left with about a hundred men and some of the women. He looked down the slope into the quarry that had been their prison for so long. Some of the slaves were still there, pathetically afraid to leave for another world they did not know or could no longer remember. A few were still working on the stones, unable to even think of doing anything else.

'Poor wretches,' Haril murmured.

'We have broken their chains,' Torm said. 'They will leave when they are ready.'

Haril nodded. His heart was heavy for he knew that the one man who should have left with them would remain behind for ever.

Chapter Thirteen

Haril knew they must rest somewhere and regain their strength. The conditions in the quarry had taken a terrible toll. It was pathetic to see how some of the slaves, even though their chains had been removed, could still not move their legs further than the shuffling steps to which the years of imprisonment had accustomed them.

Winter was fast approaching. The wind that blew down from the high mountains brought the coldness of the first snows. Haril knew it would not be long before Vardon learned of what had happened at the quarry. His warriors would be combing the countryside for them, at the same time rounding up more slaves to take the place of those who had escaped. They had to find somewhere to hide while they made more weapons and trained the men how to use them.

Torm spoke of it first as he sat with Haril, Gort, Selem and Karn around the fire on the night after their escape. The five of them were regarded unquestioningly as the leaders of the group. The others sat at a respectful distance, waiting to be told what to do, still too bemused after years of slavery to think for themselves.

'We could go to the north,' Selem suggested. 'Far enough away where Vardon cannot find us.'

Haril shook his head. 'We must be near enough to attack the temple when we are ready. And we need more men to help us. We won't find them in the north.'

'Surely there are enough of us,' Torm protested. 'As long as we have swords of iron.'

'You have not seen the temple. Vardon has many men, and those who ride horses too.'

'Your brother is right,' Selem said. 'It will not be as it was before. They know we have weapons and will be ready for us.'

Karn threw another log on the fire and turned the spit on which was roasting a deer they had caught earlier. Drops of blood and fat fell sizzling into the flames.

'There is no place near the Temple of Stone where we will be safe,' Selem continued. 'The villages are in such fear of Vardon, they would not give us shelter.'

'There may be a place,' Haril said slowly.

'Where?'

'The forest.'

The others turned and stared at him in amazement. Torm was the first to break the silence.

'None of our people have ever been into the forest,' he whispered.

'I have,' Haril replied quietly.

'You?'

'As Karn will tell you.'

Karn spat contemptuously into the fire. 'Haril is indeed a great friend of those devils who live in the forest,' he sneered.

'They aren't devils. They saved my life when ...' Haril glanced at Karn, who remained silent. It was better not to open old wounds, now that they had a greater task ahead of them.

Selem was leaning forward, eyeing Haril curiously. 'I remember the token Vardon took from you,' he said. 'Tell us about the forest people. I have also heard strange stories about them.'

Briefly, without mentioning Karn by name, Haril told of the events which had led to his meeting with the forest people. He explained what Mogan had told him of their history.

'They have the same love of freedom as we have,' he concluded. 'We need have no fear of them.'

'And yet, from what you say,' Selem murmured, 'it is our people who drove them into the forest.'

'It was a long time ago. If it is revenge they sought, would they have let me go unharmed?'

'But why should they help us now?'

'Maybe they will understand that we all face a great danger from a common enemy.'

Karn laughed sourly. 'And maybe they have bewitched you and none of what you say is true.

Maybe they work for Vardon and want you to lead us into a trap.'

'I will go into the forest alone and speak to them,' Haril retorted.

'How can we trust you?'

Haril jumped to his feet and glared angrily at Karn. 'Perhaps you will tell us just why you have cause to fear the forest people.'

'Peace, both of you,' Selem said soothingly. 'We must not fight amongst ourselves. I think we should do as Haril suggests.'

'We might be safe in the forest,' Gort said, in his blunt way. 'And if not, it is no greater than the danger we face outside.'

Torm nodded. 'I agree. We have no alternative.'

'You are all fools,' Karn cried. 'I know these people from the forest. They are devils.'

'That is old women's talk,' Haril said. 'Besides, Karn, what else would you suggest?'

'We should go as far away from here as we can.'

'And forget about Vardon and the Temple of Stone?'

'When we are stronger, perhaps ...'

Haril said contemptuously: 'Is the mighty warrior afraid?'

'Your words do not hurt me,' Karn replied. 'I fear no man.'

'Then you will come with us?'

Karn nodded reluctantly.

Selem got to his feet and looked slowly round the circle, his eyes shining with the same fanaticism he had displayed at the quarry.

'It is agreed then,' he said, sweeping his priest's robe about him with a familiar gesture. 'With the help of the god who lights the sky by day, we will destroy the powers of darkness that Vardon has brought upon us.'

There was a soft stirring as the other men edged closer towards the fire, glancing fearfully at one another. No one else spoke after Selem.

For several days they made their way slowly and cautiously across country in the direction of the forest near Karn's village. It was there, close to the place where Zia and Haril had been rescued by the forest people, that Haril hoped to renew contact with them. But as they got nearer and the forest they were skirting seemed more sinister and impenetrable than ever, Haril's apprehension increased. Suppose he could not find Zia and the old woman? Suppose the forest people killed him before he had a chance to speak to them? Suppose Karn was right after all and they really were devil-people who had put some kind of spell on him?

But it was too late to turn back now. The forest was their only refuge.

They passed Karn's village – or what was left of it. The huts had been burned to the ground and the inhabitants treated in the same way as those in

Haril's village. Haril had no liking for Karn but his heart softened when he saw the expression on the warrior's face. There was no need to ask what Karn felt. Haril touched his shoulder sympathetically: 'Your people shall be avenged.'

'I will kill Vardon with my own hands,' Karn swore.

They made camp at the edge of the forest, with many uneasy glances cast in the direction of the trees. Most of the leaves had fallen by now, carpeting the ground in a rich pattern of reds and browns and yellows, leaving the trees bare. It might have been his imagination, but every so often Haril glimpsed a slight movement in the forest and he felt, rather than saw, strange eyes looking at them.

Early the following morning he went alone into the forest. To make his peaceful intentions clear he carried no weapons, in spite of the danger of attack from wild animals. The others watched him in silence. Torm and Selem would take charge if Haril did not return within three days and would lead the group north, as Selem had originally suggested. Haril had insisted that if he did not come back, no one else should follow him into the forest.

A grey mist clung around the trunks of the great trees. It was damp and cold; the leaves on the ground were sodden and squelched beneath Haril's feet. The branches swung back behind him, as he pushed his way deeper into the forest, showering tiny droplets of dew. He had no idea which direction he should take to reach the place where the forest people lived. He just kept moving in as straight a line as possible. Every now and again he shouted out, as much to keep up his own spirits as to attract attention. His voice sounded absurdly loud as it broke the gloomy silence. A few birds rose into the air with startled cries, there were strange rustlings in the undergrowth, but no human voice answered him and after a few moments stillness returned to the forest.

It was not long before Haril knew he was utterly lost. The forest was so thick in places that he had to fight his way through creepers that hung like tentacles from the branches overhead, and so dark that he often stumbled on twisted roots and fell heavily to the ground. Soon it seemed that every part of his body was bruised and there were deep scratches on his arms and legs.

He had been walking for what seemed hours but there was no way of knowing what time of day it was. When he did come to an occasional clearing and could see above the trees, the sky was heavy with cloud and it was not possible to tell the position of the sun. It was in one such clearing that Haril took his first rest. He sank to the ground exhausted, his limbs so tired that he wondered if he would be able to stand up again. The dampness seeped into his body but he did not care. He had seen no sign of the forest people. For the first time he realised the hugeness of the forest and what little chance he had of meeting them. He had been foolish to try. If only he had listened to Karn and the others; to anyone accustomed to living in the plains, this place was accursed. The trees crowded around him on every side and in his mind he could feel them crushing him with their weight. Surely only people who were not human could live in this place. He shivered and broke out into a sweat of panic.

It was as he lay on the ground, fighting off his terror and trying to plan his best course of action, that he heard a sound nearby, a scrabbling in the undergrowth and a low grunt. He looked up, immediately alert at the sense of danger. A large boar was facing him from the other side of the clearing, its small eyes red and mean, its fully-grown tusks curving to vicious points. All tiredness forgotten, Haril rose slowly to his feet, keeping his eyes fixed on those of the animal. He had hunted wild boar often enough to know how dangerous and unpredictable they could be. But now he was not even armed with a club, let alone the flint spear he usually carried. He cursed his stupidity at entering the forest without weapons.

The boar stared at him steadily as he backed slowly towards the trees. Then suddenly, without warning, it came running towards Haril with tusks lowered, its short legs taking it faster than any man could run. Haril knew he could not reach the trees in time. He stood his ground and just when the animal was upon him, he threw himself to one side. The boar swerved past him, gave an angry snort and came at him again. This time Haril was not quick enough and the tusks caught his leg, making a raw, bloody wound. Desperately Haril turned and ran for the nearest tree, knowing he had no chance of reaching it. The memory came to him of a man he had seen gored and trampled by a boar. He could hear the animal crashing through the undergrowth behind him. Suddenly, just as it was at Haril's heels, it gave a high pitched squeal. Haril looked back quickly. The boar was rolling over on the ground, an arrow sticking from the side of its head. The speed of its charge took it past Haril until it crumbled and came to rest just ahead of him, its legs still twitching spasmodically.

Haril came to a halt, panting heavily, and looked around the clearing. At first it was just as empty as before. And then, emerging from the trees, there appeared two of the forest people. They were typically small and dark, wearing only loincloths, and both held bows with the strings pulled back and arrows pointed threateningly at Haril.

Haril slowly lifted his arms to show he carried no weapons. 'I come to you in peace,' he called out. 'My name is Haril. Do you not remember me?'

The two men stared at him uncomprehendingly and edged forward, their knuckles white from the pull of the bowstrings.

'I am known to Mogan,' Haril cried desperately.

At the sound of her name, the men glanced quickly at one another. Seeing this, Haril nodded vigorously.

'Yes, Mogan and Zia.' He pointed from the men to himself and then towards the trees. 'You take me to them.'

For a few moments the men hesitated and Haril held his breath, staring at the arrows. The men spoke to each other in their own tongue and then, after what seemed an eternity, they slowly released some of the tension of their bows. One of them beckoned Haril to follow him. The other moved to one side as Haril walked forward and took up a wary position behind him. As Haril followed the first man into the trees, he was uncomfortably aware that the second man's arrow was aimed straight between his shoulders.

They moved at a quick pace through the forest, following some kind of path although Haril could see no obvious signs of it and could not have found the way by himself. Apparently it avoided the worst obstructions for Haril found the going much easier than before. Even so, he had difficulty in keeping up with the man in front who was half running in a loping, agile gait. They plunged on through the forest in this manner, until Haril felt his lungs would burst and he could barely drag one foot in front of the other. The first man kept turning and impatiently waving him forward. Several times, Haril was nervously aware of the second man's breath on his neck.

At last, when Haril felt he could go no further and was about to collapse to the ground, they came to a steep hill. Large boulders were visible between the trees and in several places there were dark openings which led into caves. The man in front stopped and gave a high, wavering cry. The sound was echoed further up the hill. Haril was suddenly aware that more of the forest people had appeared from among the trees and were gathering around him. They were staring at him with a mixture of curiosity and hostility. The second man prodded Haril in the back. Wearily, be began to climb the hill, gaining the last vestiges of strength from the knowledge that his journey was nearly over.

Towards the top of the hill the trees began to thin out, jagged stumps marking where they had been selectively cut down. Logs were stacked in neat piles, ready for winter fuel. Then suddenly there were no trees at all and Haril found himself in an open space with nothing above him but the clouds. After the confines of the forest it was like climbing to the top of the world. A sea of treetops spread out in all directions, as far as the eye could see.

He was standing in a wide, flat plateau, in the centre of which burned a large fire. Its smoke would be visible for many miles and for a moment Haril wondered at such apparent carelessness that would reveal the location of the forest people. Then he realised that the density of the forest would prevent anyone seeing it from the ground. They were as safe from observation on top of the hill as they would be in underground caves, with the advantage of being able to observe the approach of any invader.

The group of men and women sitting around the fire were more richly dressed in woollen jerkins with furs across their shoulders and leather sandals on their feet. From the deference shown to them by the other forest people Haril guessed them to be the chiefs and elders. It was with heartfelt relief that he saw Mogan amongst them. He made his way towards the group, flanked on either side by his captors.

'I come in peace, Mogan,' he called out.

The old woman slowly turned towards him. Her face was paler and more wrinkled than ever. She stared at him and for a moment he thought she did not recognise him. He waited in trepidation while the wind blew cold about his body.

'You were warned not to return to the forest,' she said at last in a thin dry voice. 'Yet now you come with many men.'

So they had been seen after all. The eyes he had felt upon him were not his imagination. He guessed that he had been kept under observation from the moment of entering the forest.

'There is a good reason,' he said, taking a step forward.

'I hope you are right, or you may not live to see your friends again.'

'My story will take much telling and I am cold and tired.'

She beckoned him towards her. 'Sit by the fire and we will listen. Everyone here understands your tongue.'

Silently, the others made room for him. He sat down gratefully, luxuriating in the warmth that seeped through his body. Quietly and simply, he described all that had happened to him after leaving the forest. When he first spoke of the Temple of Stone, the old woman nodded.

'We know of this great temple.'

'It has become a place of evil,' he said.

In spite of the sense of shame he felt, he described his part in the building and his initial respect for Vardon. They listened without comment. But when he spoke of the sacrifice of Lileth and the strange apparitions that Selem and the other men thought they had seen, they looked at one another and murmured in low voices. As he continued, he could feel the tension mount. They leaned closed towards

227

him to hear every word he said. When he came to the death of Brond, one of the men sighed. He was bigger than the others and his hair had not yet whitened.

'Brond was a good man,' he said softly.

'His soul will rest in peace,' Mogan answered.

Eventually Haril came to the escape from the quarry and the reason that had brought him to the forest.

'We ask your help in destroying Vardon and his followers,' he pleaded. 'Before his evil spreads over all the land. No one is safe while he lives, not even you in this forest.'

'Vardon would not harm us,' Mogan said flatly.

'Others have thought that, but today they are slaves.'

'We are the only people Vardon fears.'

'Why?'

'That does not matter for the moment. Tell me, Haril, does Vardon know that you met with us?'

Haril remembered the talisman Zia had given him. He realised that Vardon would still have it in his possession.

'He took the strange piece of metal that Zia gave me,' he admitted.

There was a short cry behind him. He turned quickly and saw Zia standing there. Her face was pale and there was fear in her eyes.

'I am sorry, Zia,' he said. 'But it was not I who told him of your people, even though they tried to force me.'

'Who did then?' Morgan demanded.

'The girl Lileth,' he muttered.

'And how did she know?' Zia asked quietly. They were the first words she had spoken.

Haril could not bring himself to answer. The glimmer of a smile crossed Morgan's lips. 'There are times between a man and a woman when no secret is safe,' she said.

Haril kept his eyes fixed on the ground, knowing there was nothing he could say. For a long time, no one spoke. Then Mogan leaned forward and touched his shoulder.

'At least you have told your story with honesty,' she said.

'And will you give us refuge in the forest?'

'There is much that we have to consider. Zia will give you food while we talk amongst ourselves.'

Chapter Fourteen

Haril and Zia had been sitting for a long time without speaking. He had followed her through the trees until he could hear the sound of running water and they came to a place where the stream cascaded down from the hillside and formed a large pool. The water lapped against the bank beside them and the only other sound was the dry rustle of the wind in the bare trees overhead. Slowly, Haril leaned towards her, smelling the warm fragrance of her body, losing himself in her eyes. Then she was in his arms and her lips were soft against his and the tension and pain that was in him melted into a great wave of comfort and utter peacefulness. Her body was so small and soft as it pressed against his that he felt, if he squeezed hard enough, he could enfold her into his very being.

After a while she pulled away, her face flushed and her eyes moist. Haril took a deep breath, keeping a protective arm around her shoulders. 'I love you, Zia,' he whispered.

'And I you,' she replied simply.

For the first time, Haril knew what had really been behind his decision to return to the forest, and marvelled how he had failed to realise it before.

'In the quarry,' he murmured, remembering, 'in that terrible place, it was your face that came to me in my dreams. But somehow, when I awoke, I wasn't aware of it.'

'You must forget everything that happened there.'

Haril sighed. 'So much has happened since we met. So many things I can never forget.'

'I can help you.' She reached up and gently caressed his brow, her fingers light and soothing.

'No, I must not forget,' he said, his voice hardening. 'Not until we have destroyed the cause of so much suffering.'

He felt her body stiffen. Then she sat up, brushing the hair back from her face. 'You are right. I'm thinking only of myself.'

'When this is all over ...' he began.

'Do not speak of it now,' she interrupted. 'Do not tempt the gods. You will do what has to be done, and then there will be time for us.'

'The rest of our lives,' he murmured.

She looked at him with a gentle, half-sad smile. 'For me, it has always been for the rest of my life, whatever happened. Ever since ...' She stopped abruptly.

'Ever since when?' he asked.

'We were running from Karn's village and you waited for me to keep up with you. When you could so easily have got away on your own. I would not have blamed you.'

He took her hand and held it in his.

She stared out across the pool. 'The girl ... Lileth. Was she pretty?'

Haril had to force himself to remember. 'Yes,' he said simply.

'I am glad.'

'Listen, I want to explain ...'

'No, there is nothing to explain,' she said quickly. There was no sense of reproach in her voice. 'I am sorry she died like that.'

'And I'm sorry too ... about the talisman.'

'It can't be helped.'

'But why were you so worried?' he asked curiously. 'When I told Mogan that Vardon had taken it.'

She did not speak for a while. Then she said quietly. 'Whoever possesses it has power over me.'

He stared at her in astonishment. Such a belief in the power of personal objects was not uncommon, as Haril had found on his travels. It was often used by leaders who could only rule by fear rather than respect, or by priests who sought to enslave people by superstition. But that Zia of all people should accept it!

'You can't believe in such foolishness,' he cried.

'Not in my head, perhaps. But in my heart.'

'It's only superstition.'

'And from your time at the temple, you must know the power of superstition.'

'Only if you believe in it.'

'You sound just like Mogan. She tells me the same.'

'She's right, too. You accept everything else she tells you. Why not that?'

Zia shook her head obstinately. 'You don't understand. We will not talk of it anymore.'

'What's the talisman, anyway? I have never seen anything like it before.'

'I don't know. It is said that long ago, a pillar of that strange material was found in some deep part of the forest. My father gave it to me. He said it had been passed down through our family for many generations.'

'And you gave it to me,' he said, touched. 'Knowing that it might give me power over you.'

'You had that power already,' she answered simply.

He leaned sideways and kissed her on the cheek. 'You'll have me believing it was magic that bewitched me,' he grinned. 'Tell me – didn't your father mind you giving me the talisman?'

'He is dead,' she replied. 'He went on a hunting journey many years ago, from which he did not return.'

'And your mother?'

'She died when I was born. Mogan has always looked after me. Apart from her, I have no other family. Not anymore.'

As she spoke, Haril remembered with a sudden dread the brother she had once had. And he realised the thing he had to tell her, that he had pushed to the back of his mind because it was so difficult and he didn't know how. He got to his feet and stood at the edge of the pool, looking across at the water splashing down over the rocks.

'What is it, Haril?' Zia asked in a small, worried voice.

He searched for the right words, cursing himself for not telling her sooner, before they had committed themselves to each other.

'There's something I haven't told you,' he muttered.

'Another confession? Another Lileth?' She tried to make a joke of it, but she knew it was much more than that and was afraid.

'There's a man with us,' he continued. 'Like me, he was one of the slaves at the quarry. Zia, you must believe me; without his help, we should never have escaped. He has done wrong in the past, but ... now, he is one of us. He will fight against Vardon, and that is the important thing.'

'Who is this man?' she whispered.

'His name is Karn.'

'Karn?' She repeated the word softly with a puzzled frown as if it came from a half-forgotten dream.

'He was the leader of the men who killed your brother.'

In the end he blurted the words out coldly, almost angrily, for he could contain them no longer and could think of no other way of telling her. She gave a cry and jumped to her feet, facing him with blazing eyes.

'You have been with that monster all this time ... and you have not killed him?'

'We needed his help to escape,' Haril pleaded. 'Many lives were saved because of him. And more will be, when we fight Vardon. Does that not count for something?'

'And you would bring him to the forest, to seek our help? Traitor!' The word stung like a whiplash.

Haril felt anger and resentment rising within him. 'He has suffered and we need him now. The most important thing is to destroy Vardon and his evil.'

'If you do not kill him, then I will.'

She stood there facing him, fists clenched, her face set in hard determined lines. He knew with despair that she meant what she said.

'If we love one another ...' he began.

'You talk of love while that man still lives?' She spat the words contemptuously. 'I will seek him out now and kill him myself and my people will thank me for it.'

'No, my daughter, they will not.'

So intent had Zia and Haril been on their argument that they had not noticed the appearance of Mogan, making her way slowly up to them with the aid of a stick. They swung round to face her, startled. She looked more frail than ever, as if one gust of wind would blow her away like a dead branch from a tree.

Zia began speaking to her quickly in their own language, but the old woman held up her hand to silence her. 'Speak in Haril's tongue,' she commanded. 'This is of concern to him.'

'You know what Haril has told me, then,' Zia retorted.

'Yes, I heard. Perhaps more than I should have.'

Haril stared and could have sworn there was the twinkle of a smile in those old, half-closed eyes.

'We knew that Karn is with the men waiting for Haril,' she said.

This time it was Zia who stared at Mogan in surprise. 'And you have done nothing about it?'

'There had to be a reason for it, my daughter. I was going to ask Haril . Now he has told us both.'

'And you accept what he says?' Zia cried.

Mogan turned and hobbled over to a nearby tree-stump, on which she sat, lowering herself by keeping a firm grip on her stick.

'Come over here and sit down, both of you,' she ordered.

It was a mark of her compelling authority that they did as they were told without question. When they were seated on the grass facing her, she turned to Haril.

'First, Haril, I will tell you that the council has agreed to help you and your followers.'

Haril breathed a huge sigh of relief. 'We are all in your debt, Mogan.'

She brushed his words away with an impatient wave of her hand. 'You may camp in the forest near here and make your weapons and train your men. And when the time comes, we will send some of our own men to go with you. Not many, for we are few in number. But there are none to equal the skill of our hunters with bow and arrow.'

'And you would allow Karn to enter the forest unharmed?' Zia breathed, staring at Mogan in shocked surprise.

'You should perhaps ask why we are willing to give Haril so much help.'

'Yes, I too would know that,' Haril said. 'I cannot believe it is just for my sake.'

'You would be right young man, however well you think of yourself and would wish it to be so.'

Haril flushed, aware as always that Mogan seemed able to read his deepest thoughts, even those which he barely knew himself.

'Vardon must be destroyed,' she said.

'But why is that so important to you, who live in the forest?'

'Because the druid priests of the Samothei are of our people. We know the great power they can use if they wish.'

'How can that be?' Zia asked, bewildered. 'I have never heard such a thing said before.'

'Bah, you are like Haril in thinking nothing can be so unless you have heard of it yourself,' the old woman said crossly.

'I am sorry, Mogan. Please go on.'

'As you know, our people were here before anyone. Before time itself, perhaps. Where we came from to begin with, no one knows. That knowledge was lost long ago, during one of the times we suffered persecution and were driven into the forest. There is a legend that we came from the stars. Who knows. I sometimes think ...'

She paused and her eyes became sightless as they gazed at some inner vision. Zia and Haril sat motionless, scarcely daring to breath. Then Mogan shook herself and looked at them again.

'We had a great store of knowledge that was not known to the killers who invaded this land.'

Haril nodded.

'Long ago,' Mogan continued, 'some of our people decided to teach this knowledge to the invaders. Not all agreed. There were those who preferred to remain in the forest and live in the old way. But things always change, you see.' She sighed. 'We are the descendants of those who remained. Famine and disease and persecution have reduced our numbers to just a few. Most of the knowledge we had has been lost and it is a struggle just to survive.'

'And those who left the forest?' Zia whispered.

'They couldn't appear like ordinary human beings, or they would have been killed. So they gradually created stories to do with the wonders and magic of nature. Things which people living on the land could understand. Magic potions which were only mixtures of herbs for curing sickness. People began to visit the groves of the sacred oak to seek help, and slowly our people emerged as priests. You see, in order to teach, they had to speak in terms of the superstitions by which the people lived. They called themselves the Samothei, but were commonly known as ...'

'The druids,' Haril burst out.

She nodded. 'To begin with, they worked only for good. They taught people to live in peace, close to the ways of nature. They healed the sick and comforted the dying with a vision of life after death. Perhaps they remembered stories of that other life beyond the stars. But things change. Gradually, they came to enjoy their power over simple people. They came to believe their own myths and worship the gods they themselves had created.'

'Like the Sun-god.'

'Yes. But when, many lifetimes ago, they began to build that great henge of stone which you know so well, Haril, it was done with love and enthusiasm. To the simple-minded, it was a place to worship the sun, but in reality it was a means by which the Samothei priests could study the movement of the heavens. I don't know whether they had another purpose – perhaps to find a particular star, the place they believed they had come from. But over the years, even that knowledge became lost. The temple became an object in itself. Fear took the place of love. And now, from what you have told us and what we have learned ourselves, the final evil is taking possession. That is magic, not used to enlighten men's minds as a path to ultimate truth, but as a darkness to enslave men's souls. Vardon is of our people and we know the terrible power he can command, more than he realises himself. That is why he must be destroyed.'

There was a long silence when Mogan finished speaking. As her words burned into Haril's mind, he understood much that had previously been a mystery to him.

'Does Vardon know all this?'

'Enough to fear us if ever we should leave the forest before the temple is finished.'

'And if it is completed?'

'It would be too late. He would have complete power.'

'And what is the ultimate truth you speak of?'

'It is known to every man who has achieved complete honesty with himself and goodness of heart.'

'But you speak of Vardon as if he is close to knowing this?'

A shadow crossed her face and her eyes closed and she sat as still as death. 'There is another way to the same truth,' she murmured. 'The same degree of honesty is needed. But instead of goodness, it requires complete evilness of heart. Most men will always fall somewhere between the two and glimpse only parts of the truth. But every so often there will be one who comes to know the whole truth, by whatever path. That man will change the world, one way or the other. Either towards goodness, or evil.'

All the time Mogan had spoken, Zia had been staring at the old woman, waiting tensely as if preparing herself for what Mogan would have to tell her. Even so, when at last Mogan turned towards her, she flinched.

'What Haril says about this man Karn is right,' Mogan said softly. 'I loved your brother, as I love you. But there is a greater evil that must be destroyed.'

'So you, too, would make degrees of evil,' Zia said bitterly.

She slowly rose to her feet. 'You know that I will obey you Mogan,' she said tonelessly. 'I promise no harm will come to him from me.'

'Thank you, my daughter.'

'All I ask is that you keep him from my sight.'

'That shall be done,' Haril said eagerly.

Zia turned and looked him straight in the eyes. 'And perhaps you would honour me by doing the same.'

'Zia, please understand ...'

'I have promised because my grandmother asks me. But if you had not brought him here, if you had killed him as you should, I would not have had to make that promise. I can never forgive you for that.'

She turned and walked quickly away.

Mogan reached out a bony hand and held Haril back. She said: 'Think only of the battle that lies ahead. You must not harm Karn, however much you might want to for her sake. It would only start a feud between his men and yours, and Vardon will be forgotten.'

She turned and raised her hand towards the trees. The two hunters who had earlier captured Haril ran forward.

'They will guide you to your men, so that you can bring them back here.'

'I am grateful to you, Mogan,' Haril murmured.

He turned and followed the hunters. Before entering the forest, he swung round and took one last look at the pool. Mogan was standing there, watching him, a tiny, hunched figure who looked, with a dark shawl covering her head and draped round her body, like the withered stump of a tree that had been struck by lightning. Behind her the water tumbled into the pool and the wind brought the sound of it to him. How had Zia described it? Laughing as it splashed over the rocks, quiet and serious when it joined the pool? He choked back a cry and turned and ran with blundering steps through the undergrowth.

Chapter Fifteen

They made camp in a clearing in the forest, selected by Mogan. It was an area mainly of rocks and scrub with a few trees, so that when those had been cut down there would be open space in which the men could be trained to use their new weapons. It was close to fresh water, but not too close to the encampment of the forest people. Until the two groups became accustomed to one another, Mogan and Haril agreed that it was better to keep them apart as much as possible.

As it was, it took all Haril's powers of persuasion to bring his men into the forest. They had been brought up in superstitious dread of such regions, and it was only the greater fear of Vardon that made them agree to seek the sanctuary it offered. Karn was the most reluctant of all. He was by no means a coward but he knew that the girl who had escaped him, and whose companion he had killed, was in the forest and he was convinced she would seek revenge against him. Without naming her or revealing anything of his own personal involvement, Haril told him that she and the leaders of the forest people had promised him Karn's safety. It was one of the hardest things he had ever had to do, facing the man who had come between

Zia and himself, trying to control the anger and contempt he felt. In the end, because there was little else for him to do, Karn came with the others. But his hand was never far from his sword and he remained constantly suspicious and alert.

Winter was fast approaching and there was much to do before the winter snows came. A particular friendship sprang up between Selem and Mogan. With the knowledge that each possessed, there was much they had to tell one another, especially after the young priest learned, with great excitement, that the Samothei had originally come from the forest people. Haril could not help feeling a pang of jealousy when he saw how much Mogan confided in Selem. As the weather became more severe, she was unable to leave the warmth of the caves, and that was where Selem also was usually to be found. He told Haril sadly that it was not likely that she would be able to survive the winter. The forest people did not have a single leader, but were ruled by a high council to which Mogan belonged. When any of them died, their place was taken by the person to whom they had imparted their knowledge, which might be one of their own children or anyone else they had chosen as suitable. In Mogan's case, the cloak would pass to Zia.

Only once, during the building of their camp, did Haril catch a fleeting glimpse of Zia through the trees. He called out to her, but she disappeared as quickly as a startled fawn. Anger at the unfairness of it overcame Haril and he vowed he would not again go to the caves where the forest people lived. He kept his promise, but the anger could not sustain itself during the lonely, restless nights, and it soon evaporated, leaving him morose and unhappy. Torm was the first to speak of it and asked him what was wrong but Haril refused to remind himself of Zia by talking about her, even though she was seldom far from his thoughts.

Gort took charge of training the men for the battle that lay ahead. The huge warrior, with his lusty appetites and zest for life, his bawdy jokes that would be accompanied by bellows of laughter, his temper which was as quick to fall as it was to rise, was liked by everyone. He himself did not know where he had been born. At an early age he had been bought by Vardon's men and trained as a warrior, finally being given the honour of joining Vardon's personal bodyguard. It was the only life he knew and he revelled in the sweat and thrill of battle. More than anyone he appreciated the strength of the iron swords and took every opportunity of showing what feats could be achieved with them, from hacking down trees to digging pits in the ground, over which the shelters were built.

But the revelation came when he first brought some of the forest people into his motley army. He had tended to treat them with good-natured contempt until the day when they demonstrated their little bows in the open clearing where he had established a training area. He had set up targets made from animal skins at which Karn's men were shooting with their own long bows. Some of the forest people were watching impassively, including one of the hunters whom Haril had first met in the forest and whose name, he later discovered, was Malk.

'Let us see what you can do, little men,' Gort shouted boisterously.

Malk and two of his companions glanced at one another, then walked over to the firing line which had been marked out on the ground.

'Let them move twenty paces forward,' Karn called out, smirking. 'We don't want their little arrows blunted by falling short on the ground.'

The little men did move – not forwards though but further away from the target. There was a stunned silence as they measured out another fifty paces, bringing them close to Haril's hut, then a great roar of laughter.

'You're meant to hit the target, not Haril's hut,' shouted one of Karn's men.

'Perhaps they use those little bows to throw at the enemy to trip them up,' cried another.

Ignoring the remarks, Malk fitted an arrow to the string, pulled it back with a quick aim, and fired. His companions followed suit. The arrows sang through the air in graceful curves and landed within a finger's length of each other in the centre of the target. The laughter died down as everyone stared in astonishment. Malk went over to Gort, the suspicion of a grin on his lips.

Gort shook his great head as if not believing what he saw. 'You did that ... with those little bows?'

'It is not the bigness, but the bend of the wood. See?' Malk held out his bow. Gort took it gingerly and tried to pull back the string. In spite of his strength, he could not pull it as far as Malk had.

'It takes time to learn,' Malk said apologetically.

Gort clapped a bear-like arm round his shoulder. 'You shoot like that at Vardon's men and we won't even need swords.'

Malk took out one of his arrows and fingered the pointed flint that was bound to the shaft. 'Bad thing, the head sometimes breaks,' he said. He looked at Gort's sword. 'If we could have metal like that ...'

'Why not?' Haril had come up to them now and was staring at the arrow. 'There's no reason why we can't make iron arrowheads.'

Gort clenched one mighty fist and clapped it thunderously into the palm of his other hand. 'By the gods, I think we'll beat them yet.' He turned to Malk. 'Come on, little man, we'll see how you are with a sword.'

They marched away, Gort shouting to his men to take up their swords. Haril stayed where he was, thinking deeply; they would need many more swords, and now arrowheads as well. The problem was to find a source of iron ore. Haril had already spoken of this to Mogan, but she had not known where it might be found. There was nothing like it in the caves where they lived. However, she had told him of another area of rocks and caves several days' journey away. He would lose no time in going to investigate.

Gathering some supplies together and selecting several of the forest men to guide him through the forest, Haril was soon ready to make the expedition. He decided that it would be safer to make the weapons at the place where they found the iron ore, rather than make them at the camp.

*

Selem arrived at the camp soon after Haril had left. The priest wore an expression of deep sadness. Torm knew that something had happened as soon as he greeted him.

'It's Mogan,' Selem said heavily. 'She is dead.'

Torm recalled Haril's affection for the old woman. 'Should we tell Haril and bring him back?'

Selem considered for a moment, then shook his head. 'There won't be time. We are asked to go now, to attend her burial. Besides, I have a feeling she preferred him not to be there.'

Torm raised his eyebrows. 'I thought there was friendship between them.'

'That is so. I was with her at the last, and she has given me a message for him. No, it is some other reason. I do not know why.'

'Then we will go, with Gort and Karn. To show our respect.'

'She was a wise and gentle woman. She will be sadly missed.'

Karn was reluctant to visit the encampment of the forest people, but after a warning glance from Gort, he agreed. The four of them, together with all the forest people who were in their camp at that time, set out through the forest.

It did not take them long to reach the caves. Even before they arrived they could hear a low, mournful dirge that was like the wind when it blew strongly across the plains. When they reached the rocky plateau, the burial ceremony had already begun; the members of the high council were gathered around a kind of raised platform, on which was placed the body of Mogan, dressed in white. A blue cloak, similar to that worn by the councillors, was draped over the platform. Gathered on the slopes leading up to the plateau, except for the one side where it dropped down abruptly in a steep cliff overlooking the forest, were several hundred of the forest people, more than Torm had ever seen at any one time. In answer to his whispered question, Selem told him they had come from other camps and were all that remained of the forest people. Then Torm understood the reluctance they had shown to allow more than a few of their men to join the fight against Vardon. They were in threat of becoming a dying race.

One of the elders began speaking in their strange tongue, his melodious words accompanied by more keening from the women. Then the stretcher was lifted from under the cloak and taken to the edge of the cliff. For a moment, Torm thought they were going to throw the body over the edge. But when he moved over to the cliff and looked down, he saw that a hollow had been scooped out on a narrow ledge some way down. Some of the forest people had climbed down by ropes, and now helped to guide the stretcher as it was carefully lowered. The body was placed in the hollow, then carefully and with great reverence one of the men took a large rock and broke the bones of Mogan's legs and the neck behind her head. With the limbs now free to move, her legs were drawn up and her head pushed forward until she assumed the position of a baby before birth. Ornaments and bowls of food were placed in the grave, then it was filled with stones until they were piled up in a small mound above the level of the ledge. Thus Mogan reached her final resting place, facing far across the forest that had been her home.

Karn turned away impatiently, thinking the ceremony was now over. But it was not. No one else moved, so there was no way of pushing through the crowd behind him. He faced the platform again and saw that the cloak had been taken away by two of the elders and was now being put across the shoulders of a slim dark-haired girl. As he stared at her, his heart suddenly pounded within him and his hands began to tremble; he recognised her as the girl who had once been a prisoner in his village, before Haril had taken her away. The events of that night, not long ago in time but seeming to belong to another life after all that had happened since, flooded back into his memory. He had killed her companion and tortured her. Now, she had obviously been made one of the leaders of her people. And Karn understood a leader to be someone who could command anything he or she wished; such as the life of the man who had made her suffer.

It took all Karn's courage to stand there, feeling that she must be staring at him, waiting for the right moment to raise her hand and order her people to seize him. He closed his eyes, seeing in his imagination the knives plunging into his body. But nothing happened. When he opened them again, it was apparent that the ceremony was over. The people were drifting silently away, the girl was standing with the elders, her back towards him.

'We must go and speak with her ...' Selem was saying.

But Karn had already turned and was thrusting his way down the slope.

Gort, who had no great liking for Karn, gave a short laugh. 'He does not like to be reminded of death.'

But Torm frowned and shook his head. 'I would swear it is not that. It seemed to have something to do with the girl. I was watching him.'

After they had approached Zia and greeted her, Torm said: 'There was another with us. Karn. He regrets that he had to leave before greeting you.'

He watched closely for her reaction and was sure that the flicker of some emotion showed itself in her eyes. But what it was, he did not know.

*

Karn ran desperately through the forest, blundering into trees, tripped over the undergrowth, scarcely aware of the direction he was taking. It was more by luck that he found himself back in camp. His first thought was to flee, putting as much distance as possible between himself and the girl who must surely seek her revenge against him, now that she had the power to do so. But where could he go? The trails through the forest were no more than a maze to him; he would never be able to find his way out. His next thought was to gather his men together and prepare to fight. But they would have no chance against the larger numbers of the forest people, and he doubted whether his men would be prepared to sacrifice themselves just for him.

Not knowing what else to do, he went into his hut, took his sword in hand, and waited there like a trapped animal. But, as the moments went by, there was no sound of men coming to take him. After a while, Torm, Selem and Gort returned, talking to each other amiably as if nothing had happened. Karn squatted down on the furs that made his bed and furiously tried to think. Maybe they would wait until night. But for what purpose? Maybe she was just playing with him, tormenting him by waiting and then suddenly seizing him when he least expected it. That seemed more likely. But gradually, another thought came to him. Of course. From what Haril had said, the forest people wanted to destroy Vardon. And to do that, they needed Karn and his men. The more he thought about it, the more sense it made. She would make use of him and then, when it was all over, would be the moment for her to take her revenge.

A feeling of relief came over him. He put away his sword and went to the door. All was peaceful outside, the women cooking over the camp fires, some of the men practising swordplay as Gort had taught them. He was still in danger, but now he was aware of it. He had time to think. Time to plan his own course of action. He smiled grimly. Had he not always been known as the most cunning hunter in his village?

*

It was some weeks before Haril returned with his small party, laden with the implements it had made. It had taken them some time to find the kind of rock which contained the iron ore, but once they had done so, Haril had excelled himself. In addition to many swords he had made arrowheads and even axes, shaped like the ones of stone he used to make, only far stronger. With practise at cooling the weapons with water and then reheating them he had become skilled at sharpening the edges. Gort was so delighted, as he brandished one of the swords, that he almost succeeded in cutting off his other hand.

There were days during the worst part of winter when blizzards raged through the forest and they had all sat huddled in their huts, wrapped in furs, striving to keep the fires alight, and grumbling about the foolishness of their venture. But slowly the weather became warmer and the snows began to melt, overfilling the rivers with rushing torrents. The days lengthened, and as the hunters went once again into the forest, there was fresh meat cooking on the spits and a new feeling of enthusiasm in the air.

Haril worked and joked and feasted as enthusiastically as any of them, more so, in fact, for it was easier to pretend and it was only when he was alone that his heart was heavy. He had not seen Zia all winter, and now he doubted if he ever would. When he had heard of Mogan's death he felt sorrow, but he was honest enough to admit to himself that it was more because of Zia than the old woman. Now Zia was more remote from him than ever before.

As spring approached, the time came when Haril knew they would need more precise information about the Temple of Stone before they could make further plans. The forest people had shown a remarkable ability to find out what was happening in the outside world. In some uncanny and unexplained way, messages travelled through the forest faster than a man could run; although few in number, the forest people seemed to have outposts everywhere. It was in such a way Haril learned that Vardon's men had restarted work at the quarry, after rounding up more slaves, and that his warriors were still searching the countryside for those who had escaped. Many in fact had been recaptured, and Vardon had offered a large reward to anyone who brought him the ringleaders.

It was essential that they should find out what stage had been reached in the building of the temple. Haril remembered with cold dread what Mogan had told him: Vardon would achieve the ultimate power when the temple was finished. It was said that the final stones would be put in place by the summer. Other rumours, never spoken aloud but whispered furtively from one mouth to another, told of things strange and sinister at the temple that brought chill terror to all who heard. Haril knew that time was running out for them. 'Someone must go to the temple and bring us word of what is happening,' he said when the five leaders were discussing the problem one evening.

Gort shook his head vigorously. 'It would be madness,' he growled. 'We will make our attack when we are ready and trust to the gods, and our swords of iron.'

'We must know the best moment to strike,' Haril insisted. 'And since I know the place, I will go.'

'And I will come with you,' Selem added quickly.

Torm looked aghast. 'You'll never get out again. I agree with Gort. It is too dangerous.'

'That seems to be two against two,' Haril said. He looked across at Karn. 'What do you say Karn?'

Karn frowned, as if pondering the question, but Torm thought he could detect a sly grin on his lips.

'We do need information,' he said at last. 'I would go myself if I knew the place. But for Haril and Selem, I think it would be worth the risk.'

And so it was settled and no amount of arguing by Torm and Gort could dissuade Haril.

Chapter Sixteen

Before they left on the journey to the Temple of Stone, Haril and Selem had to attend a final meeting with the high council of the forest people. It was a moment Haril dreaded, for Zia would be with them and he would see her face to face for the first time since they had parted at the place beside the pool.

The two men were dressed as shepherds, which was how they hoped to enter Vardon's camp. There was a constant coming and going of such people for there were many mouths to feed and produce had to be brought in from the hills and farms around. They carried no weapons. If they were caught they could put up little resistance anyway, and they didn't want any of the weapons of iron falling into Vardon's hands. But Selem insisted on wearing his priests' robe under his rags. He felt there might be an occasion to use the immediate authority it conveyed.

The councillors were gathered together in one of the caves. The plan of action had already been agreed. Malk would guide Haril and Selem through the forest to the point where it came closest to the temple. This would still leave them the journey across open country to reach the site. Unless he heard to the contrary, after seven days Gort would lead all the others to the same point at the edge of the forest and await word from Haril and Selem. They planned to make a surprise attack just before dawn, approaching the temple under cover of darkness.

As Haril stood before the high council, he scarcely heard a word of what was being said. He had eyes only for Zia. She looked more beautiful than ever, her hair falling in black waves about her shoulders, contrasting with the sky-blue of the cloak she wore. Beautiful, but withdrawn, and with an unmistakable sadness in her eyes. When it was her turn to speak, there was a tremor in her voice.

'I will pray that both of you return safely,' she said gravely.

Selem said: 'I have vowed to live until I see the Temple of Stone fall to the ground.'

'And vows should be kept.' She looked at Haril.

Haril clenched his fists. 'Many vows are made in haste,' he said angrily. 'But perhaps they are not worth keeping.' He glared at her for a moment and then turned abruptly away.

'Will you not say farewell?' she whispered, so quietly that even Selem, standing beside her could barely hear. And maybe Haril didn't hear at all for he continued to walk away without looking back. Selem saw tears in Zia's eyes and took her hand in his. 'I don't know what is between you two,' he said gently, 'but I will make sure he returns.'

'Thank you, my friend. Make sure you both return.'

*

The forest was coming alive with spring. Leaves were unfurling into a fresh green splendour, small animals played joyously among the branches, and even the bears were pushing their snouts out of their winter lairs, testing the warmth of another year. Everywhere there was activity and birdsong. As Haril made his way through the forest with Selem and Malk, following ancient trails, he marvelled that it had been a place he had once feared. Even in the gloomiest depths there was beauty. There was danger as well, of course, but the more Haril knew of the forest, the more he felt at one with it. The open plains now seemed bleak and bare to him, the stone villages unfriendly. It would have been different had his own village existed. But it did not. He had no home.

The journey was long and arduous. Occasionally, Haril had the feeling that there were other people near them, following perhaps. At last they began to leave the denser areas and came to where the trees were more widely spaced and sunlight cast dappled shadows on the mossy ground. There came a moment when Malk, who was leading them, turned and held up his hand to indicate caution. They crept forward stealthily and suddenly there were no more trees ahead but open country unfolding before them.

Haril and Selem had been so long in the forest, where one could seldom see further than a few paces away, that they had to blink to bring their eyes into focus. It was another world to see so much sky again, not just a glimpse of it overhead between the trees but such a vast expanse that different kinds of weather were visible at the same time, cloud and rain in one place, blue sky and sun in another.

Far away, slightly below their level and on a rise in the middle of a bowl-shaped plain, stood the Temple of Stone. From that distance the stones did not look particularly imposing. But what did seize the imagination was the myriad of tiny ant-like figures swarming over them and dotted over the surrounding ground. Haril's heart sank; he had forgotten just how many there were in Vardon's vast army. It was true that most of them were slaves or workers, who it was hoped would rise up against their masters once the attack began. But from his experience in the quarry, Haril had his doubts about how much help they could expect.

Closer to them were tilled fields and the poor huts of peasants. Sheep were grazing on the hillside and they could just hear the thin notes of a flute being played by a shepherd boy who sat on a rock with his back to them. The sound stopped suddenly, and Malk urgently signalled them back into the trees. Galloping along the side of the hill came a small party of Vardon's horsemen, the sun glinting on their bronze helmets and shields. With shouts of laughter they rode through the flock of sheep, scattering them in all directions. And then they were gone.

'It was just a patrol,' Selem whispered. 'I don't think they were looking for anyone in particular.'

'Maybe they have helped us,' Haril replied.

'How?'

'Look over there.'

Several of the sheep had trotted up the hill towards the trees where they were hiding. The boy was some distance away, trying to round up the rest of them. Haril took out his knife and pointed to the sheep. Selem nodded. Together with Malk, and looking quickly from side to side, they crouched down and made their way slowly into the open. It was only a matter of seconds to seize two sheep and kill them with a quick knife thrust to the throat. Malk picked up some stones and began throwing them at the rest, until they turned and trotted back down the hill. Haril and Selem dragged the dead animals back into the shelter of the trees.

Standing up again, Haril saw that the shepherd boy and all the sheep had disappeared to the other side of the hill. If he and Selem went in the opposite direction and then circled round towards the temple there was little chance of the boy seeing them. Nodding to Selem, he hoisted one of the sheep on to his shoulders. There was no point in waiting; now was as good a time as any.

Selem picked up the other animal and together they turned to face Malk. The little man reached out and lightly touched their hands. 'I wait here for you,' he said.

'Thank you,' Selem said. 'Take care you are not seen.'

Malk grinned. 'No one sees a forest man if he does not wish it so. But it is you who must be careful.' He watched them go with a heavy heart. He could still see them plainly when, after taking twenty paces or so, they turned and looked back at the forest. But they did not see him.

In spite of the weight on their shoulders and the detour they had to take, Haril and Selem made good progress. It was not long before they were on the main track leading to the temple. The stones loomed up much larger now, stark against the skyline. Both of them felt a dryness in their throats and a deep sense of apprehension. Occasionally they passed people moving in either direction – peasants, workers of various kinds and women with yokes across their shoulders carrying water. They kept their eyes fixed firmly on the ground, fearful to look another in the face. The two men copied the attitude of the other passers-by, depressed at the atmosphere of despair around them but glad of it because no one wanted to ask questions. They were just two more serfs who owed their very existence to Vardon. But perhaps there was not enough humility in their attitude, for when three of Vardon's warriors came riding out of the camp, sweeping those on foot aside into the ditches, it was beside Haril and Selem that they pulled up their horses and stopped.

'Where are you two going?' one of the men shouted.

Haril bowed low. 'We bring meat to sell in the camp,' he said, trying to match the whining servility of a slave.

The man stared at him in astonishment. 'Sell?'

Selem glanced up, saw the expression and thought quickly. 'My friend is simple and tries to joke, Master,' he said apologetically. 'We bring meat because it is our honour to serve you ... and the soldiers told us to.'

One of the other men laughed. 'That was old Set and his men, I'll wager. I saw him riding up to the hills earlier.'

The first man still seemed suspicious. 'Why have you killed them, then?'

'It is quicker to carry than to drive them, Master.' Selem answered. 'Sheep are such stupid animals who do not always go where they are led.'

'Like your friend here, eh,' the man grinned, giving Haril a kick that sent him staggering across the path. 'Let's have no more talk about selling. That was before the Dark One came.'

The other two men glanced uneasily at one another. 'We must be on our way,' one of them muttered. 'Unless we want to be here when the sun goes down.'

The soldiers looked back at the camp and Selem would have sworn they shivered. Without another word, they turned and rode away. Selem walked forward to join Haril, who was staring after them angrily.

'Keep your head lowered,' Selem urged. 'You're supposed to be a serf, don't forget.'

'I won't forget if I meet those three again,' he said. 'And what's this about me being simple in the head?'

'You are, if you don't do as I tell you.'

Mumbling under his breath, Haril bowed his head and they continued along the path.

As they came nearer to the Temple of Stone, they were aware of a heaviness in the atmosphere that was like the time before a summer storm. The people all about them moved as if in a dream, with staring sightless eyes and leaden feet. When he had been at the site before, in spite of the cruelties, Haril remembered that as evening came and families gathered together, one would hear the sound of laughter and the shouts of children playing around the fires. Now there was no laughter and sounds were muted into a dull, lifeless murmur, only occasionally broken by an angry or despairing cry.

Even the guards seemed affected by fear. In fact, when they came to the area where men were working on stones and at various other crafts, there was much less bullying and whiplashing than before. But in its place was something worse. A total surrender of body and soul to the will of another.

Haril didn't dare to look up directly at the temple, for even that action would have been out of place in that bowed, shuffling mass of humanity. He sensed that Selem felt the same, and also kept his eyes averted. But there was no denying the presence of the massive stones; they loomed over them like black thunderclouds, casting long, chill shadows that seemed to suffocate all in their path.

Dusk was beginning to fall by now, and they were able to merge more inconspicuously with the crowd. But as they came to a section near the temple which had been cordoned off by wooden posts, a guard standing by the gateway grasped hold of Haril.

'Is that food for us?' he grunted.

'We were taking it to the other side ...' Haril began, but the man pushed him towards the fire that was burning in the middle of the compound.

'It's ours now,' he said, without emotion. 'The other one too. See it's cooked properly or I'll roast you with it.'

Selem followed Haril over to the fire. There was nothing else they could do. But as they squatted down and began skinning the sheep, they realised it was an ideal situation for their purpose. They could work without notice or interruption and study the temple at the same time. Most of the guards had not yet returned and except for the man at the gate, the compound was deserted.

At first glance, the temple looked much as it had before. There was still scaffolding round some of the uprights and ropes connecting one to the other so that the men could move about without having to climb down to the ground and then up again. But as Haril looked more closely, remembering the plan, he saw that it was indeed nearly finished. Around the outside was a ring of tall, slender pillars, joined overhead by flat slabs of stone, broken only to form the main entrance. Inside, in a series of diminishing circles, were the more massive monuments, leading to the centre where the biggest of them all was positioned. What stunned Haril was the fact that, in spite of the tangle of wood and ropes about some of them, all the arches had been put into place except on the centre pair of uprights. Of course, as he knew, Vardon's plan would not be completed with the building of the temple. He had an ambitious scheme to build an entire city on the sloping ground outside. But it was the temple that was his dream, and it looked as if he was very close to achieving it. In the centre, between the altar and the sighting stone which was positioned to catch the first rays of the sun when it rose over the distant hills, the last huge arch stone lay on the ground, ready to be lifted on to the uprights. When that was done, the temple would be complete.

'Do you see, Selem?' Haril whispered.

Selem nodded. 'Vardon will wait for the day that marks the end of winter and the beginning of spring.'

'That's little more than a week away.'

'Quiet.'

Selem bent down over his work, and Haril heard the thud of approaching footsteps. The guard came and stood beside them, watching as they tore off the last of the skin and inserted long bronze skewers into the carcasses so they could be turned as they roasted over the fire.

'It must be ready for us to eat before the sun goes to rest,' he said gruffly.

'Yes, master.'

'No one is very hungry afterwards.' The guard seemed to be talking more to himself. He looked down at Haril. 'Have you come far?'

'From the hills,' Haril pointed vaguely towards the forest.

'And have you been in the temple at night before?' The guard spoke in a tone that was almost friendly.

Haril gave Selem a quick glance, then shook his head. 'No, master.'

'When you've finished here then, go as far away from this place as you can, before the sun goes down.'

Selem couldn't resist asking the question. 'Why, master?'

'Because you'd see things you wished you had not. Now get on with your work.'

The guard strode away abruptly, as if he regretted having spoken.

Soon, the other men began to appear; they were silent and morose. A few came across to the fire and watched the fat sizzling on the meat as Haril and Selem turned the spits.

'It doesn't do much for your appetite,' one of them muttered.

'Don't think about it,' said another. 'Just thank the Dark One it won't be you.'

'There are more tonight, then?'

'So I hear.'

'What for?'

'They were found praying to the Sun-god.'

The others looked, horrified, at the man who had spoken.

'You risk your life by saying that name,' muttered on of them, turning away.

No one spoke after that. When the meat was cooked, the guards took out their knives and began slicing off chunks to eat. Selem signalled to Haril and silently they moved away. None of the men took any notice of them. When they were outside the compound, Haril turned to leave the camp. Selem took his arm and held him back.

'We should go now,' Haril whispered urgently.

Selem glanced at the sun, which had sunk nearly to the horizon, and then looked around the camp. There was a strange feeling of expectancy in the air; people were drifting slowly and silently towards the temple, as if drawn by some force beyond their will.

'I want to see what happens,' Selem murmured.

'It's too dangerous, Selem, come on, we've found out what we came for.'

'You go, if you wish.'

Haril frowned with exasperation. Every moment they were in the camp, they were in danger. But he couldn't leave Selem on his own.

They joined the people moving towards the temple. Going through the wide entrance, past lines of guards standing stiffly to attention, Haril marvelled at the symmetry of the stones. They were placed in such a position that wherever one stood, the eye was drawn compellingly towards the altar in the centre. Beside it was Vardon's large tent, now sheathed in golden silk. On the other side was stacked a pyramid of brushwood and logs, the fuel for a fire as yet unlit. But strangest of all were three wicker-work baskets suspended over the fire from a long crossbeam. They were like large versions of the dolls that peasants made for their daughters to play with, stuffed with straw and with crude faces painted on cloth heads. The figures swayed gently in the breeze, pieces of straw protruding from the extremities of their arms and legs which stuck out rigidly like scarecrows. Haril wondered where he had seen such effigies before, and then remembered they were sometimes burned during celebrations in the villages, to ward off evil spirits it was said. He saw to his relief that the altar stone was bare.

By the time the setting sun touched the rim of the hills, everyone in the camp had gathered around the temple. The altar priests and leading warriors were gathered behind the altar, forming a line from Vardon's tent. Everyone was staring silently at the entrance. At last the flaps were pulled aside and a figure appeared.

Haril had expected to see Vardon, dressed in white like the other priests. He was totally unprepared for what did emerge from the tent and moved across the clearing to stand behind the altar. The body was that of a man, dressed entirely in black with a cloak that swirled like the wings of a bat. From the shoulders up was the head of a goat, but one much larger than that of an ordinary animal; it stared ferociously over the crowd, teeth bared, horns curling up from a shaggy mane, black eyes glowing in the sockets that seemed to pierce the heart of anyone who looked on them. Haril drew back, and heard Selem take a sharp intake of breath.

It seemed that the eyes were staring straight at them, knowing them for who they were. Haril had only once before seen eyes like that. But was it Vardon behind the mask? Reason told him it was so. But there was something so intensely real about the massive head that he couldn't be certain.

Bathed in the eerie orange light of the dying sun, the figure raised its arms and began to speak. And again, it could have been the muffled voice of Vardon, deep and utterly compelling, but perhaps not. Everyone was rooted to the ground, as motionless as the stones around them, all strength sapped from their bodies. Haril could barely make out the words, so awed was he by the sound itself, and many of them seemed to be in a strange tongue. Afterwards, all he could remember was some kind of prayer to the Dark One who came with the night, conquering the sun, and that the time would come when the sun would be destroyed and never appear again. It was the ultimate blasphemy to the Sun-god and all that the priests had previously taught. Haril took a quick glance at Selem and saw that the blood had drained from his cheeks and his shoulders were trembling.

A large bowl was placed before the figure, which it lifted to its mouth, and drank deeply. It was too dark now for Haril to see very clearly. As if in answer to his thought, one of the priests stepped forward, holding a lighted torch. He threw it on to the fire. The flames took hold immediately, casting flickering shadows amongst the stones. By their light Haril saw with horror and disgust trickles of red liquid running down the hairy chin of the goat-figure. It had been drinking blood. The priest who had lit the fire bowed low before the figure, then turned to the crowd.

'Witness the fate of those who dare to call on the Sun-god, who is merely the servant of the Dark One.'

All eyes turned towards the basket figures dangling over the fire. It seemed to Haril, as tongues of flame began to lick their straw feet, that they made a slight movement. As the fire crept higher the strange jerking motions became more pronounced, like puppets dancing from strings. And then the full realisation came to Haril and his stomach heaved sickeningly. Inside each of the baskets, arms and legs tightly bound by straw, was a man. As more of the straw caught fire, the blackened limbs began to show themselves, kicking and twisting grotesquely. They made no sound until the final moment, when flames reached the straw that had been thrust into their mouths. As it turned to cinders, slightly faster than the flesh for it was dry, high pitched screams tore the silence. Then, with an explosion of sparks and smoke, the baskets with their charred remains crashed down into the fire, and the silence returned.

But not for long. Another loud cry rang out, not of pain but of anger. With a horror that froze the beating of his heart, Haril saw that Selem had wrenched off his shepherd's rags and was shouting like a man seized with madness.

'It is Vardon who blasphemes,' he cried, pushing forward through the crowd. 'It is Vardon who wears the mask of the goat and brings evil to this place.'

The shock of his outburst was so great that no one could move, Haril least of all. He watched aghast as Selem ran up to the altar and faced the crowd, his arms held high.

'You know me,' he cried. 'I am Selem, priest of the Samothei. And I say to you that the Sun-god is the one true god and he will tear these stones to the ground. You worship a false god. Vardon deceives you by his evil.'

Selem swung round and pointed accusingly at the goat-figure, which stood motionless. 'I call on you to reveal yourself, Vardon. Let us see you for what you are.'

Such was the force of Selem's anger and the authority he commanded that no one made an effort to restrain him.

'Do you not dare to reveal yourself, Vardon?' Selem shouted again.

The crowd stared at the goat-figure, stunned and hardly able to comprehend what was happening. Haril shrunk back. But as the moments passed and

Selem repeated his taunts, Haril suddenly became aware of a change taking place among the crowd. Voices began to murmur, there was a slight movement forward, and with amazement he sensed that anger and hatred was overcoming fear. Incredible as it seemed, Selem had a chance of succeeding. If all the slaves and workers rose up, forgetting their fear, they could easily overpower the guards and priests. And even some of the guards were glancing uncertainly at one another, for the first time doubting the power of Vardon.

Haril pushed his way forward, opening his mouth to take up Selem's cry. He knew that others were on the point of following him. It only needed one or two to start running forward, and Vardon could be swept aside, defeated by the very people he had ruled with such cruelty, by the superstitions he himself had created.

And then it happened, just as Haril was about to shout out. No one knew where he came from, but suddenly Vardon was standing by the altar, next to the goat-figure, dressed in his white and gold robe.

The goat continued to stand motionless. So certain had Haril been that Vardon was behind the mask that for a moment it seemed that he had merely removed it from his shoulders. But the figure was there to bear witness that this was not so.

Vardon looked at Selem, who stood transfixed, unable to speak.

'I am here, Selem,' he said in a voice that was soft yet reached to every part of the temple. 'And now, like me, you will bow to the Dark One.'

Selem stared at Vardon, then at the goat-figure behind the altar. Vardon bowed low to the figure. Quietly at first, then louder, a wail of fear broke out from the crowd. They fell to their knees, Haril among them, for he too was caught up in the terror of the moment.

When at last Haril dared to look up, he saw that the goat-figure had gone. Vardon stood to one side while the guards led Selem unprotestingly away. There was nothing that Haril could do. With despair in his heart he drifted away with the others, matching their shuffled steps and dreamlike stares – feeling, indeed, much as they did. It was perhaps the shock of what had occurred that lent reality to his pretence of submissiveness, enabling him to wander without hindrance away from the camp and back to the hills like a simple shepherd who had witnessed the birth of a new world.

Chapter Seventeen

All through the winter, when the weather permitted, Gort had been training his little army for the battle ahead. From an ill-assorted group of farmers, weavers, hunters and the like, he had fashioned a body of fighting men whom he would have pitted against the best. Gort and his own warriors were armed with iron swords, which they had learned to use with great swinging blows, in a way that was impossible with bronze implements, and they carried shields of the same material. Some of the more robust plains people, such as Karn's hunters, also had swords, but most bore long spears which were intended less for throwing than for warding off Vardon's horsemen. Finally there were the forest people whose arrows, tipped with iron heads, had become deadly weapons.

The time had now come to make final preparations for the march through the forest, to meet with Haril and Selem at the place agreed. The men were packing their weapons and supplies of food into bundles to carry on their backs. Gort was striding amongst them, exchanging crude jokes, giving a word of encouragement here, a growl of criticism there. Suddenly, Haril stumbled into the clearing, followed by Malk. Both looked exhausted, their clothes torn and muddy. Gort ran to join them.

'We must speak,' Haril muttered wearily.

While the men glanced anxiously at one another, wondering what had happened, Gort led them to a hut where Torm was packing up his own possessions. Quietly, and without emotion, Haril told them what had taken place. A long silence followed his words.

'I am sad for Selem,' Gort said, shaking his head. 'He was a good man.'

'They'll kill him, of course,' Torm said.

Haril lowered his head. 'Not immediately. Vardon will want to know about us.'

Torm stared at him. 'Surely he will not tell them?'

'Selem will not speak,' Malk insisted.

Haril shrugged. 'I pray you are right. But how can we be sure? He would not know the way to lead them through the forest. But he knows how we plan to attack.'

'And without surprise, it will not work.' Gort said grimly. 'The weapons of iron are not enough by themselves.'

They sat in silence, each filled with despair. Haril was torn by conflicting emotions. One part of him wanted to run blindly at once to attack Vardon, knowing that every moment lost meant more suffering for Selem. But another part still felt the chill fear of that night, after he had left the temple, when he had lain trembling on the ground and it was only Malk's comforting words that had given him the strength to move. The urge was strong in him never to go near the accursed place again.

Trying to forget his fears, Haril looked round and suddenly realised that Karn was not with them.

'He's probably hunting,' Torm said in answer to his question. 'He's been gone for several days.'

'He should be here,' Gort growled. 'We are soon to leave.'

Malk got to his feet. 'We must ask our high council,' he said firmly.

'You are right,' Haril nodded. 'I wish we had Mogan's wisdom to help us ...'

The elders heard them with growing unease. When they had finished, one of them said: 'We must move at once to another part of the forest. We are no longer safe here.'

'Have you forgotten Mogan's vow to fight Vardon?' Haril cried. He looked around for Zia, seeking her support, but could not see her. 'We must find another way of attacking the temple.'

They began speaking amongst themselves, in their own tongue. It appeared there was a disagreement, but finally one of them turned to him.

'We agree, Haril. But we must send the women and children to safety. If you do not succeed, Vardon will surely seek to kill us.'

'And Zia will go with them,' Haril said quickly. 'But I do not see her with you now.'

'She has not been here for some days,' the man said with a worried frown. 'We thought she might have waited in the forest for your return.'

Malk shook his head. 'We did not see her.'

'Then where is she?' Haril cried, jumping to his feet.

Torm hesitated, uncertain whether or not to speak. Haril saw his doubt. 'What is it, Torm?'

'I didn't realise ...' he began slowly, 'but I suspected. Karn ...'

Haril gave a loud cry of despair, remembering what Torm had said earlier. Karn had also disappeared. And he knew that Zia had been right. He should have killed Karn when he had the chance. It had been foolish to trust him. He should have realised that being the kind of man he was, cunning and untrusting himself, he would never believe in anyone else's trust. And now – had he killed her? Taken her prisoner? Terrible images raced through his mind. And he remembered other things. The impression that someone had been following them through the forest. It might have been Karn, seeking to learn a way out for when the time came.

Quickly, he told the others the first meeting between Zia, Karn and himself. The forest people knew, of course, but they had respected Mogan's wishes that Karn be treated as an ally.

Haril seized the hilt of his sword. 'We must search for them,' he cried.

One of the elders held up his hand. 'We have ways that are faster.' He turned to Malik. 'Send messages to our people.'

For the rest of that day, written signs were passed on by a succession of arrows to various parts of the forest. At last, as evening fell and Haril felt he could contain his impatience no longer, the answer came. Karn and two of his men had been seen leaving the forest, close to the point where Malik had waited for Haril. They had Zia with them – and they were heading towards the Temple of Stone. One of the messages also told of a large party of slaves from the quarry heading in the same direction, carrying stones that were obviously intended for the city that Vardon planned to build. The knowledge held no interest for Haril as he sank to the ground with a groan. He scarcely heard the words, such was the despair in his heart. But Torm listened, and a thoughtful look came into his eyes.

*

Selem lay in the miserable, foul-smelling hut into which he had been thrown after his capture. That first night, Vardon had come to gloat over him and demand to know about his companions. The beating had gone on for hours, until he passed mercifully into unconsciousness; he had not spoken, but he was terribly afraid that he might do so when the pain became too great. To his surprise, however, they had left him alone the next day, and the following night. Now it was the third day, and when suddenly he heard the sound of approaching footsteps, he braced himself for another ordeal. There was probably some savage purpose in leaving him so long, letting his mind dwell on the cruelties to which he might be subjected.

The door opened and light flooded into the dark prison. Vardon stood in the doorway, his long face wrinkled in distaste at the smell. 'Bring him outside,' he ordered.

Two guards took hold of Selem and dragged him out. They were in an area behind the temple, close to where the priests had their tents. Selem could even see the tent in which he had lived, a large stone-floored structure of animal skins held in place by wooden stakes and ropes.

'You see, you have not moved such a great distance since last you were here,' Vardon said sardonically.

'Not so far as your evil has taken you, it seems,' Selem retorted. It was the first time since his capture that he had seen Vardon clearly, in daylight, and he was shocked at the transformation that had taken place in his appearance. Vardon's face had always been gaunt, but now the chalk-white skin was stretched so tightly it seemed that the bones underneath would break through the brittle covering. Dark shadows circled his eye-sockets. It was like looking at a skull. Except for the eyes. They still glowed with the inner power that Vardon had always possessed, but now they showed a hint of something else, not the fanaticism of his earlier years but something at once more subdued and more evil. They spoke of some terrible knowledge which should not have been in the power of man to comprehend. Selem shivered. He felt he was in the presence of something more than the man who was Vardon.

'Are you not pleased with the work here, now that you have seen it?' Vardon said. 'Are the stones not magnificent? And much of it was due to your help!'

'For which I pray to be forgiven. This is a monstrous place, Vardon. I will not rest until it is torn to the ground.'

Vardon laughed. 'You think your friends will help you?'

'You cannot make me betray them.'

'No? Not the impetuous Haril? Quiet Torm, who thinks before acting? That ruffian Gort, and the little forest man – Malk do you call him?'

Selem stared at Vardon in astonishment. 'I did not tell you those names.'

'Perhaps you did. In your sleep – or in pain. Do you think their weapons of iron will really overcome all the warriors I will be able to send against them?'

A guilty flush spread over Selem's cheeks. Vardon watched with amusement.

'It is surprising how a man forgets what he has said under such circumstances. The attack in darkness, for instance, just before dawn on the last day of winter. It is to be made from the edge of the forest, I believe.'

'Stop!' Selem cried. 'I would not have told you knowingly. Rather would I cut out my own tongue.'

'An interesting possibility. But I would not lose the pleasure of your conversation, Selem. You were always one of the more intelligent of my priests.'

'They are not priests any longer. You have made devils of them, like yourself.'

'Really Selem. You always said such things were superstition. Are you not so sure, now?'

'I know you are capable of anything, Vardon. But why this way? You could have achieved what you wanted through the path of light.'

Vardon shook his head. 'You know that is untrue. Free men do not work as slaves do. The temple would not have been finished your way.'

While Selem held Vardon's attention, his mind was feverishly trying to recall what he might have told Vardon. Had he given away the whole plan? Could he make Vardon believe he was lying? Suddenly he caught Vardon's eyes, and knew with a sinking heart that the high priest could tell exactly what he was thinking.

'I will put your mind at rest,' Vardon said. 'You did not betray your friends. But here are two you may wish to meet.'

He turned and made a signal. A moment later Karn appeared, leading Zia by the arm. She was deathly pale. Selem gave a cry of astonishment. Zia ran over to him, while Karn knelt before Vardon.

'You are hurt, Selem,' Zia whispered, looking at the bruises on his face.

'It doesn't matter. Why are you here?'

'Tell him, Karn,' Vardon ordered.

'I serve the Dark One, and Zia is the prize I brought him,' Karn said.

'And a very important prize, for which Karn will be well rewarded,' Vardon said with a smile of satisfaction, looking at the girl. 'I could not have wished for anyone better than Mogan's granddaughter for my purpose. Now there is no one in the world who can stop me, not even the forest people.'

Selem stared at Karn. 'Then it is you who betrayed us,' he cried. He would have run forward and seized him by the throat, but the guards held him back.

'You should thank Karn,' Vardon said. 'By telling me your plans, he has saved you much pain.'

Selem struggled like a man with madness. Zia went up to him and put her hand gently on his shoulder. 'Be still,' she said quietly. 'They will only hurt you more.'

Selem heard her words through the rage that was in him and slumped back in the arms of the guards. Sorrow and despair overwhelmed him. Vardon had won after all. He would know what Gort intended, and be ready for them when they came. They wouldn't have a chance.

'I see you understand,' Vardon murmured. 'That is good. It pleases me that in your last hours you should know my triumph.'

'Do with me what you will,' Selem said. 'But you do not need the girl, now. Let her go.'

'That is not possible,' Vardon replied, shaking his head. 'You will both play an important part in the greatest work of all. Come, I have something to show you.'

Vardon led them through the temple, under the great stone arches, and finally to the altar in the centre. He pointed towards the most massive uprights of them all. Selem looked up. Workers were preparing to put the final arch-stone into position. The scaffolding, built in the form that Brond had devised so long ago for Haril, had nearly reached the top. The logs groaned and creaked under the enormous weight of the stone, but they would clearly hold.

'You know what day it is tomorrow?' Vardon asked.

'The last day of winter,' Selem replied. 'The day that celebrates the coming of the sun that will bring us life and warmth this summer.'

'So it has been in the past. But when the sun fades at the end of that day, the last stone will be put in place and the temple will be completed.'

Vardon's voice trembled with emotion. 'And then will begin a ceremony such as the world has never seen before,' he whispered. 'I will not tell you the nature of your deaths. They will be more terrible than you can ever imagine. But out of your suffering, I shall call to the Dark One. And he will appear among us, to be Master of us all. Do you hear? The Dark One will rule the world, and I shall be his servant.'

Vardon raised his arms towards the stones and gave a mighty laugh that brought dread to those who heard.

'Then what was that creature the other night?' Selem demanded.

Vardon smiled cunningly. 'It is sometimes necessary to trick those with feeble minds. It fooled you for a while, I think. Long enough for my purpose. But tomorrow night will be no deceit. The birth of the new year will see the final triumph of the powers of darkness.'

Selem felt as if a cold hand had clutched his heart. Looking at Vardon, at the power that even now emanated from him, Selem could not doubt that he spoke the truth. For himself, Selem preferred death to living in a world ruled as Vardon intended. He felt a great sadness for Zia, who was standing silent and pale beside him; for her, and Haril and all the others. But perhaps it would be better for all of them to die before this terrible thing came to pass.

Vardon stood motionless, deep in thought, and it was as if a dark shadow had fallen over him, so that his outline was not clear but blurred and a dark mist seemed to hang over his head. Then he closed his eyes and when he opened them again the mist and shadows faded and he looked around him, slightly puzzled, as if he had returned from a long journey.

Karn stepped forward and bowed before him. 'Before that great night Master, we must defeat Haril and his people.'

Vardon nodded slowly. He turned and led the way through the temple until he was standing at a point where he could see across the plain to the hill where the forest began.

'Before it is light tomorrow,' Vardon told them, 'your friends will come down from the forest, expecting to take us by surprise. We will allow them to come into the open. And then, Karn?'

Karn pointed to one side where a group of warriors were grooming their horses and polishing their helmets and shields.

'The horsemen will gallop between them and the forest,' he explained. 'And when our warriors on foot come out to meet them, they will be surrounded.'

'There will be no survivors,' Vardon ordered casually.

'That is understood, Master,' Karn replied, casting a gloating look at Zia.

'It should provide a minor entertainment, before we are concerned with more important matters,' Vardon continued. 'And since it will be your last day, Selem, you may watch my triumph with me.'

'May your soul be damned,' Selem cried.

Vardon smiled. 'It is you who will suffer that fate.'

'You can do what you want with my body. But my soul is mine.'

'We shall see,' Vardon said grimly. 'What if I tell you that your pain will be so great that, as the only means of finding a merciful death, you will be willing to inflict that same pain on the girl? And that will be your last act on earth.'

Selem stared at him. 'What do you mean?' he whispered.

'You have a lively imagination. I will leave you to consider the possibilities for yourself. Now, take them away, I have much to do.'

The guards seized hold of Zia and Selem dragged them away. Selem saw Zia being pushed into one of the huts, then he was thrown inside the place where he had previously been held prisoner.

*

During the long hours of that day and into the night, Selem lay on the damp floor with utter darkness enveloping him like a shroud. However much he tried to concentrate his mind, he could not keep out unbidden images of a thousand terrible tortures and deaths. He knew Vardon too well and had seen enough already to know that it would be more horrible than a mere mortal could devise. But what terrified him even more was the knowledge that Vardon's power over him could extend beyond the grave; if he did as Vardon intended, and subjected Zia to the same suffering, he would be damned forever. Even when a restless sleep came, the visions remained, jumbled with those of dreadful and nameless apparitions, until he woke screaming, the sweat pouring from his body. But there was no respite, for the darkness was as black as in sleep. And as he stared about him it seemed that one particular image, which had haunted his dreams, was still there. The image of a human face with blood-red eyes and fearsome teeth and a scaled, slimy body, crouching somewhere in the hut, waiting to leap at him. And as terror took complete control of his mind, it came to him that even death would not end his suffering but would only be the beginning.

Chapter Eighteen

When at last the guards came for Selem, an hour before dawn, he was huddled in one corner, his eyes wild and staring, muttering feverishly to himself. The guards looked at the demented man, then at one another, uncertain what to do. But Vardon had given the order and to disobey was unthinkable. They reached down and each took an arm and carried him outside. His limbs were as rigid as those of a man who had been dead for a long time.

Gradually the cold night air soothed the heat on Selem's brow and cleared the blackness that had overwhelmed his mind. Movement came back into his body and he was able to walk. He looked up and saw the stars in the sky and a half-moon slipping towards the horizon. After the horrors of the past hours he was numb, beyond fear even. He felt only a total resignation for what was to come.

Vardon, Karn and Zia were already standing on the area of high ground outside the temple. Selem looked at the girl and saw from her eyes that she had experienced something of what he had been through; they smiled sadly at one another and touched hands. Hers were like ice. Vardon glanced at them and then turned away and continued looking slowly over the camp. No one spoke.

Everywhere was bathed in a pale, silvery light. It shone on the massive stones, making them seem even taller than they were, and caught the sides of the tents and huts that were all around them, reaching away into the distance until they were lost in shadows. Here and there glowed the dying embers of a fire. Beyond the camp a heavy dew had fallen over the grassy plain, reflecting the soft moonlight. Further away the upward slope of the hills showed clearly, and only where the forest began was there blackness. At first it seemed that the camp slept and all was still. But then Selem began to detect faint sounds, carried by the gentle night breeze. The tinkle of metal on metal. The murmur of voices. A horse whimpering and pawing the ground. As his straining eyes became more accustomed to the darkness, he could see the occasional movement of shadows in that area of the camp facing towards the forest. Some distance away, to the right, there was a larger shadow which he took to be the group of horsemen, waiting below the line of the forest. And the scene was peaceful no longer, but charged with the atmosphere of many men awake and alert, preparing to do battle.

Vardon was staring at the hill where it sloped down from the forest. Selem looked in the same direction, creasing his eyes. At first, everything seemed normal. And then, so imperceptible that it might have been his imagination, he saw tiny figures moving out of the forest. Had they not been expected, no guard on sentry duty would have seen them and the surprise they intended would have been possible. Even as he watched, the moon disappeared behind the cloud and the light gradually faded, leaving that darkest time before dawn. The figures were no longer visible; but all knew they were there, walking straight into Vardon's trap. For one wild moment, Selem had thought that Haril might have changed the plan, even decided not to make the attack after all. But now that faint hope was dashed. He glanced round at Zia, and saw that she was silently crying. There was nothing he could say to help her.

'We must welcome your friends,' Vardon said, smiling. 'You wait here. Karn and I will attend to the preparations.'

When they had gone, Zia turned to Selem. 'Do they have a chance?' she whispered.

Selem shook his head. 'The swords of iron were important, but surprise was the real weapon. They are one against a dozen. But it will be an honourable death.'

'And quick,' she added in a small voice.

Selem put his arm round her shoulder and whispered close to her ear so that the guards could not hear. 'At the right moment, when fighting has started, we will run from here, towards Vardon's warriors. With their blood roused by the battle, I think they will kill us. It will be better that way.'

She nodded. 'I shall be proud to die with Haril.'

The minutes went slowly by and then suddenly, to the east, the sky began to lighten. Vardon and Karn returned and they all stared as this new light, so different from the false dawn, stole across the plain. Karn gave a grunt of excitement and pointed. Faintly they could make out the figures that had come down the hill. They were bigger now, more than half-way towards the camp and spread out in two wavering lines. Far behind them, at the top of the slope near the forest, horsemen were galloping in a long column to cut off their retreat. When the signal was given, they would charge down the hill while the foot soldiers, lined up just outside the camp, marched forward. Haril and his men would be caught in the middle, in open ground.

A pile of brushwood had been placed beside Vardon. Firing it would be the signal for the two groups to move. It was rapidly becoming lighter now, and the pleasure of anticipation showed on Vardon's face. He took a torch from one of the guards and walked over to the fire. At that moment, another guard appeared and knelt before him.

'The slaves with stones from the quarry are approaching, Master,' he said.

'Do not trouble me now,' Vardon snapped. 'You know where they should go.'

The guard went away. Selem glanced to the other side of the camp. A long, bedraggled line of slaves was making its way along the track towards the main entrance. They carried on their shoulders large stones that would later be used for building the city Vardon planned. Overseers stood by, whipping them on their way.

'It is time,' Vardon announced triumphantly. He thrust the torch into the brushwood; the flames flared up and with a loud shout, the foot soldiers began running forward. Far away, they could just see the horsemen turn and begin their long ride down the hill. Selem gave a deep groan.

Because of the way the land outside the camp rose and fell into a slight decline, Haril and his men would remain hidden for a while from the sight of the soldiers. But from the position Vardon had chosen, on a high piece of ground by the temple, there was an unimpeded view of the battlefield. As the sun broke above the horizon, and visibility suddenly improved, Selem strained to distinguish between individual figures. What he saw he was at first unable to believe. Instead of men armed for war, the figures that emerged in the dawn of light were sheep, several hundred of them, spread out across the fields, urged forward by a few of the forest people. Vardon gave a strangled cry. Selem stared at the scene in astonishment. Vardon's foot soldiers were running forward, shouting and brandishing their weapons, but not yet able to see the enemy. His horsemen were charging down from the hill, in their case still too far away to see properly. But all that both groups would find when they met in the middle was a large flock of sheep.

Selem threw back his head and gave a roar of laughter. Vardon, his face twisted with rage, drew back the torch that he still had in his hand and would have smashed it against Selem's head. But at that moment, there came the sound of shouting from another direction, close to the main entrance where the slaves were approaching. As Vardon and all those with him turned, they saw the slaves dropping the stones and the overseers throwing away their whips. And with a great surge of exhilaration, Salem recognised Gort and Haril and Torm and all their people. They had taken hold of weapons concealed under the stones and were streaming into the camp, cutting their way through the few soldiers and guards who had not left with the rest to do battle on the plain. It was just at that moment that the two parties of Vardon's warriors met and realised with cries of anger how they had been tricked.

Gort had planned the operation well. By the time that the main force of Vardon's army came running back towards the camp, he had positioned bowmen along the perimeter, one line kneeling in front, another standing behind. The enemy was met with a seemingly continuous hail of arrows as the two lines shot alternately. They fell back in disorder, leaving many dead and wounded. Meanwhile, in the camp area, a fierce fight was raging. The horsemen, seeing the devastating power of the bowmen, galloped around to the main entrance. But once in the camp, which was now in utter confusion as the workers ran to and fro in panic, knocking over tents and fires, it was difficult for the horses to manoeuvre. There was no advantage in being on horseback, as Gort had foreseen when he chose the camp as the battlefield and not the open plain. Those warriors who stayed mounted found themselves at the mercy of long lances before they could reach the men who held them. Soon, everyone was fighting on foot. And it was now that the real battle began, as iron met bronze, the superior advantage of one equalling the larger numbers of the other.

*

As soon as he had taken hold of his sword, Haril had tried to fight his way through to the temple, driven by the thought of Zia and what might have happened to her. But it was some time before he could get anywhere near. Occasionally he would find himself close to one of his friends – Gort shouting loudly with delight as he wielded the huge sword that had been specifically made for him and which no other man could lift, Torm using his lance to hold off two of the enemy, thrusting forward and then darting back before they could reach him with their swords. And then there would be a surge of bodies and they would be parted again. Once, he caught a glimpse of Selem, high up on a scaffolding, seemingly binding ropes around one of the stones. But there was no time to wonder what he was doing. And there was no sign of Zia – or Vardon.

Then suddenly, Haril was face to face with Karn, and iron met iron for the first time. Karn fought like a man possessed, for he knew he could expect no mercy. One of them had to die. Haril found himself being driven back, then, summoning all his strength, advanced with savage thrusts and blows until they had reached the temple. Their swords clashed together and then against the stones with deep, ringing echoes. A blow from Karn caught Haril's shoulder and he could feel the blood trickling warmly down his arm. He lunged forward, then as Karn went to parry the blow, changed the direction and stepped sideways. Karn saw the movement too late. Even as he lifted his sword, Haril swung down and struck Karn at the point where his neck met his shoulder. A glazed look came into Karn's eyes, his sword clattered to the ground, and he fell back, dead.

At that moment, above the raging battle, Haril heard a shrill cry. He swung round, his chest heaving, his arm so heavy he could barely lift the sword. Behind the altar stood the goat-figure, dressed entirely in black, the curved horns and bared teeth catching the pale rays of the morning sun as it rose above the sighting stone. But this time he knew it was Vardon who wore the mask. Vardon held the sacrificial knife high in both hands. One of the guards was pulling Zia backwards across the altar, baring her white neck and bosom to the knife. Haril knew he would not be able to reach her in time. Desperately, gathering what little strength he had left, he grasped the blade of his sword and threw it at the guard. It caught the man full in his chest and sent him staggering backwards to collapse on the ground. Zia slipped and fell from the altar stone, just as Vardon plunged downwards with the knife. It missed Zia by a finger length and struck bare stone.

'Quick ... over here, Zia!' Haril cried, running back and picking up Karn's sword. Zia scrambled to her feet and came towards him.

A deep, muffled voice filled the temple. 'I command you, in the name of the Dark one, to come to me.' It was Vardon who spoke. In one hand he grasped the knife. In the other, held up so that the light glinted on its surface, was Zia's talisman which Vardon had taken from Haril.

Zia, in the act of flight, saw the talisman. She stopped and stared. Vardon beckoned to her again.

Drawn against her own will, she took a hesitant step towards him.

Haril's throat was so dry, he could hardly speak. 'No! No!' he cried hoarsely. 'Don't listen to him, Zia.'

She stopped, still staring at the talisman. Haril knew that if he moved, Vardon would get to her first. Vardon called her yet again. Suddenly, with a sob, she turned away and came running towards Haril. Vardon made a move to pursue her but the altar was in the way and he was only halfway across the temple when she reached Haril's outstretched arm. He held her for a moment, keeping the sword pointed at Vardon, then gently pushed her behind him and began walking slowly forwards. Vardon backed until he was at the altar, then raised his arms and began screaming words in a strange tongue. As they poured out of the snarling mouth of the mask, it seemed for a terrible moment as if it was an animal itself which spoke. The sound rose higher in a blood-curdling shriek and the men who were fighting outside paused and stared at each other in horror, friend and foe alike. Haril felt the strength draining from his body, the sword weighing heavier and heavier. His will was being taken from him. However much he fought against it, he knew that the sword would fall from his hand and he would stand helpless before the high priest.

And then there came a cry from overhead. So compelling was it that both Vardon and Haril looked up. Selem was standing on the last arch-stone that was waiting to be placed in position. The scaffolding that held it up had reached the top level of the uprights.

'Watch, Vardon,' Selem shouted. 'Watch the destruction of your temple.'

Selem held a lighted torch in his hand. He leaned down and thrust it against the wooden scaffolding. As the timbers began to burn, he threw the torch to the bottom so that the scaffolding would catch fire there as well.

At first, Haril didn't understand. When the scaffolding burned and then collapsed, all that would happen was that the one stone which it was holding up would crash to the ground. But then he saw something else. Selem had tied thick ropes around the stone and connected them with some of the key uprights. As the stone fell, its enormous weight would pull these over. They in turn would fall against other stones.

Vardon had seen as well. With a cry of anguish, he ran towards the scaffolding where the flames were now fiercely catching hold. For a fleeting moment, he had forgotten Haril, intent only on cutting the ropes. Haril leapt forward and with a mighty blow, severed the head of the goat from Vardon's body. It rolled forward, blood spurting from its neck. Haril had a sudden horrible impression that it was not just Vardon's head inside the mask but that the two had become one. But there was no time to find out. The wood was well alight now, and the stone was beginning to fall.

Selem was still standing triumphantly on the arch-stone. The smoke was beginning to billow up around him. If he stayed where he was, he would either be burned to death or be crushed when the stones collapsed.

'Cut the ropes,' Haril shouted. 'Then climb on to one of the other stones until we can get you down.'

Selem shook his head, a wild look in his eyes. 'The temple must be destroyed,' he cried.

In spite of all that had happened, Haril once again felt a desperate urge to save the stone from destruction. He, of all people, knew the skill and knowledge that had gone into the building as well as the suffering.

'Vardon is dead,' he called out, urgently.

'There would be others seeking to make use of the evil of this place.'

'But you will be killed.'

Selem fell into a fit of coughing as the smoke blew into his face. 'Pray for the day when one who is of the light and sun will be born to the world,' he cried hoarsely. 'Now run quickly ... before it is too late. And take Zia with you.'

Haril turned and saw Zia leaning against one of the stones, deathly pale, her eyes closed. As he ran to her, the weight of the arch-stone was beginning to pull on the others. Slowly, with a terrible groaning sound, they began to move from their foundations. Haril lifted her in his arms and carried her to the edge of the temple. When he looked back, Selem was scarcely visible through the smoke. But for a moment it was cleared by a gust of wind and Haril could see the young priest clearly. He was facing the sun with his arms outstretched, bathed in a golden light, seemingly oblivious to all that was going on around him. Then he disappeared completely behind a wall of flame.

Haril stepped back until he was a safe distance from the temple. Behind him, the fighting had stopped. Everyone was staring with awe and fascination at the great henge of stones. There was a loud crash as the scaffolding collapsed. Then a deep roar as the stones began to fall, one pulling down another until the very earth trembled. As they cracked and splintered into a thousand fragments, a huge cloud of dust and smoke arose and hung in a pall over the temple, as if shielding its destruction from the sight of mere mortals, for this was where the gods would have lived. There was no sound from those who watched, not even a shout of jubilation from the victors. They felt only shock and a sense that all of them had come out of some terrible nightmare and the world was theirs once more, still a place of good and evil, perhaps, but at least there was a choice to be made.

Haril felt Zia stirring in his arms and looked down to see her smiling at him. He set her carefully on her feet and together they looked round at the camp. Most of it had been wrecked, the tents pulled over, small fires smouldering among the ruins of the thatched huts. Vardon's men had laid down their weapons and were sitting on the ground, nursing their wounds or just staring into space. The workers and slaves were wandering amongst the wreckage with dazed expressions, unable yet to comprehend fully what had happened. Malk was gathering his forest people together, searching for those who were dead or wounded. Torm was with a group of priests who had survived, talking to them earnestly and, Haril guessed, probably making plans already as to where they should lead their people. Gort was sitting on a pile of logs, tying a piece of cloth round his leg where he had been wounded.

From far away came the melancholy notes of a flute, played by one of the shepherds coming down from the hills to see what remained of the temple that for so long had dominated their lives. For the rest of time perhaps, people would come and stare silently at the ruins, wondering what had lead men to build it in the first place. But Haril and Zia, as they moved forward to meet their friends and prepare for the long journey into the forest, did not look back.

About the Author

In a varied writing career, Bryan Cooper has been a journalist, author, and screenwriter. Starting as a reporter on a local newspaper (the *Bromley and Kentish Times*) on leaving school at 16, he went on to work in Fleet Street before joining the press department of British Petroleum as feature writer on the company's worldwide activities, including Middle East oil developments and the early days of exploration in Alaska and the North Sea. BP's sponsorship of motor racing led him to cover all the major international races and rallies in the heydays of the late 1950s, writing for a variety of newspapers and magazines. With the publication of his first book in 1967 – *The Ironclads Of Cambrai* – he left to become a full-time writer, publishing books on military history and other subjects. His fiction writing included short stories, radio plays, and scripts for such TV series as *No Hiding Place* and *The Troubleshooters*. For some years he edited and published the international energy magazine *Petroleum Economist*. Bryan Cooper was born in Paris, where his father was foreign correspondent for *The Times*, and after a lifetime of travelling and living abroad now lives in the Kent coastal town of Deal with his wife, Judith Windsor, the well-known film and theatre voice coach.

4934973R00181

Printed in Germany
by Amazon Distribution
GmbH, Leipzig